<u>DEDICATIONS</u>

*This book is dedicated to the people whose
hearts and hands held me up through my
darkest hours. You cried when I cried, and
celebrated all my victories when I was
victorious. My never-ending love and gratitude
I extend to my Husband for his prayers, to my
daughters for your camaraderie, and to my God
for extending me the miracle of life.*

I0200597

You Can Get There from Here | Pat Martin

"There is no phase of the maze that can hinder you from reaching your ultimate destiny."
Pat Martin

You Can Get There from Here | Pat Martin

TABLE OF CONTENTS

Chapter 1:
"The Health Maze" (pg. 1)

Chapter 2:
"The Wealth Maze" (pg. 43)

Chapter 3:
"The Relationship Maze" (pg. 89)

Chapter 4:
"The Spiritual Maze" (pg. 131)

Chapter 5:
"The Emotional Maze" (pg. 181)

Chapter 6:
"The Journey" (pg. 225)

Chapter 7:
"The Way Out" (pg. 259)

You Can Get There from Here | Pat Martin

FOREWORD

This book you're getting ready to read is about a woman who is indispensable to me. She's my Mom, my muse, and best friend. I am also her guinea pig for costumes in stores, and impromptu lunches when we should probably be working. We eventually get back to work in time though.

Over the years, I've watched my Mom work tirelessly as a Registered Nurse, compassionate wife, and still give my sister, Melody, and me 110%. This superwoman would preach, teach, pick up students, lead praise and worship, put on major stage productions, write grants, invest her time, money and energy to underserved youth in our community, and just simply give of herself continuously. Unbeknownst to many, she suffered from a condition, Achalasia, that caused a stricture in her esophagus where she may not even be able to swallow a drop of water. This could go on for days with no food or nutrients in her body. I would feel so sorry for my Mom, but persistent and strong was she.

The day had come that I found myself—along with my Dad and sister—being escorted to a consultation room in the hospital. The Dr. informed us he wasn't able to do the surgery; in addition to there being a bigger concern. The

unfathomable news had been broken. A lump
was found on her esophagus, and it may be
cancerous. As I write this now, I'm feeling an
overwhelming emotion of sadness. Tears are
slowly filling my eyes revisiting how
devastating this day was.

Moments up to that week, I'd been
touring the world as a musician and spent a lot
of time away from my family. They certainly
have a great deal to do with how strong I am;
especially my Mommy. Being uncertain, I
couldn't begin to imagine her fate. Thoughts of,
"Well I haven't accomplished this and that, I
haven't gotten married yet, I haven't had
children." All the things that I would want her

to see and experience with me rushed through my mind all at once. Feeling shattered, I put my big girl face on as I headed to see my Mom in recovery. I remained as strong as I could. The year 2016 just seemed to be spiraling down paths with no outs and this was yet another one.

There we were, standing around my Mom's bedside as the doctor disclosed this information. Just witnessing her initial response was indicative of the fortitude she possessed. Seemingly, I think she did better than me. That somehow made me want to cry even more. Over the next six days as we awaited the results, I watched this woman in her resilience find ways to keep going; even with the uncertainty of a life-threatening illness. Were there difficult times for her? Of course, there were; however, they never seemed to overshadow the light at the end of the maze. I gleaned a sense a strength from her that I never knew existed. My Mom held onto her Truth knowing this lump could indeed be cancerous, but she embraced her hope with vigilance. By far, it seemed like the longest week, but today I'm grateful to God for the conclusion of the matter!

So, if you're wondering why I deem Pat Martin to be competent of helping you get through your maze, it's because I've witnessed firsthand the strength, the courage, and the wisdom that exuded from this woman. This ultimately got her through her own maze. I believe this whole experience took place—not just for my Mom's sake—but for the benefit of those that seek guidance from someone who is selfless and honest; and from one who has been in her own maze of uncertainty. To say I'm proud is an understatement. I love my Mommy to no end, and will forever hold onto these values in all I aspire to do. And what's more, I wish the same for you too. Wherever your *here* is, this book is sure to help garner results and motivation to get you to your *there*.

Sincerely,

Tracy Martin

World-Renowned Musician

You Can Get There from Here | Pat Martin

INTRODUCTION
"YOU CAN GET THERE FROM HERE"

Making it through the mazes of life can be an extremely difficult thing to master. By mazes I mean the extremely meandering roads and paths one must embark upon to get to their greater calling and destiny. The journey is different for everyone, but you can rest assure that the journey will have complications; and it will at times feel like you're lost in a maze. However, as you walk down the winding roads of life you will find that it's not impossible to get *there*. You *can* get to the light at the end of your tunnel.

This book was written to help give you guidance through the mazes of health, wealth, your emotions, relationships, and your spirituality. It is the purpose of this book to help one strategize through each maze, and to empower you to your ultimate destination.

To understand the complexities of life is usually far beyond one's human intellect. It would take the omniscience of God to even begin to obtain just a bit of understanding. But one thing's for sure, the walls of our maze serve a twofold purpose. On the one hand, they may be obstacles causing us to take unexpected detours; or they may serve as protective devises that safe guard us from unseen dangers.

Little did I know as I took the journey
through each maze my pains would direct me
and propel me to my purpose. One thing I've
learned as you're walking down the roads of the
mazes of life is this; you do not go through the
mazes without a cause and a reason. Although
the reasons may not be readily revealed, you
will soon gain insight as to what God is really
trying to get out of you; and *where* God is really
trying to take you.

I am convinced that my journey has not just
been for me, but for the empowerment of others.
Everyone's maze is different, yet everyone has a
goal to reach. I pray that as you are reading this
book you will clearly see that there is no phase

of the maze that can hinder you from reaching your ultimate destiny in life. Although there are no straight and narrow ways to purpose; you can still get *there*. Know this one thing for sure, where there's a will, there's a way. You *can* surely get there from here! *If you're ready to walk, read on.*

You Can Get There from Here | Pat Martin

You Can Get There from Here | Pat Martin

1

<u>The Health Maze</u>

The architect who designed the building must have been using the blueprint of a maze. "Take the elevator to the second floor so you can get to one. The first floor will put you on third, and the third floor will put you on the ground floor outside. Believe it or not you can get there from here." It's just like life, full of mazes. There is no direct path to greatness and every street leads to yet another twist and turn most of which cannot ever be anticipated. Just when you think you've got it down pat and know the way, you run right into another turn. That turn leads you into unfamiliar territory again. Quickly you come to the place of confusion. "Where am I? Where do I go from here? Wait a minute, Déjà vu. I'm sure I've been here before. Going around in circles soon becomes the norm until you can find an opening in the maze, the opening that takes you to the next place of uncertainty. How ironic that the name they use for childbirth classes is "Lamaze". So very apropos for the journey the child will make throughout the rest of their life.

The health maze is the journey that usually begins with everything intact and in its rightful place. Everything is well until age and gravity come together in a meeting of the minds. The two sit and discuss what area of chaos they can cause today. Now did I mention that there are two other factors sitting at the table? Those factors are Stress and Hope. What most folks don't realize is that Stress and Hope have the greatest influence during the health maze.

Age and Gravity

Age and Gravity starts on a happy trail in the maze of health. They set foot in the maze on a usual path then along comes Stress entering the trail. Stress then often steps ahead of Age and Gravity and begins to lead the way. Oh, I forgot to tell you that Stress is blind so he walks into every wall he encounters. The difference—

however—between Stress and Hope is that Stress walks *into* walls where Hope walks *through* walls. If Stress is leading the way you'll see that he wanders to and fro like the devil himself. He seeks what body part or system he can destroy. His job is to carry the weight of Life whether they are financial, marital, employment, discouragement or other emotional influences. After so long the stressors of Life will become too heavy to carry around. At this point Stress lays them down on one of the body parts, systems, or organs.

In my case he laid them down on my esophagus. It was as close as he could get to my heart. Once Stress securely laid it there, then I began a tumultuous thirty year battle through the health maze. "Ugggh" is probably the best word I could use to describe this journey. A maze it was! It seemed that each time I made it through one level or obstacle course; it only turned out to be another brick wall or entrance to another part of the maze.

Let the Health Maze Begin!

Over thirty years ago I was working as a registered nurse in a hospital in Tallahassee, Florida. The hospital was right near the college where I had just graduated with a BS degree. Ironically my education and degree were not enough to keep me immune from disease. How ironic it seems that a doctor or nurse should ever be sick. I went to school to heal the sick, not to be sick. Nevertheless, on many days I found myself suffering. It started one day at work when I felt myself having some difficulty swallowing. I immediately pulled out my *rationalization card* and assumed I was drinking too much coffee, but the coffee cessation did not make a difference. Later I pulled one of the gastroenterologists aside and whispered to him, "I think I need to come see you." I never wanted to cross the professional lines with the Doctors by having them consider my personal health matters, but it was necessary. He at least tried to protect my privacy by placing me on a hospital floor away from the same nurses I had to work with every day.

May I just take a moment to do the unthinkable and break hospital code? You must know that Doctors and nurses discuss patients outside of the professional setting all the time. It's a coping mechanism for them—or should I say us—to deal with the stressors of the medical profession. So, to avoid me being the topic of discussion among my peers the safety of distance was put in place.

Now, during that hospitalization the Doctor had no clue of what the problem was. So, I ended up just getting a much-needed vacation. Little did I know—however—I was just about to enter the bowels of my health maze that I had never anticipated.

As time passed the problem grew progressively worse. I found out what it was like to eat normally one day then go for weeks without being able to even swallow water. This is no game. It's just a matter of time before you become too weak to function. Someone should have given me an Oscar over the years. As sick as I was, I relentlessly continued my work on my job, in ministry, and around the community. Everybody knows the universal sign for choking is to place your hands around your throat. Well I would just keep my hands on my stomach pretending my stomach was uneasy or something. I would hold on to my stomach while I was teaching, preaching, or serving in the community, run to the bathroom to vomit, and then run back to my task never skipping a beat.

Please forgive me for having to use the unsavory word *vomit,* but it became the story of my life. All day every day. Sometimes it happened several days in a row, *uggh.* I have often gone three weeks without being able to swallow a meal. On bad days, even water would not pass through the tightness in my chest. My children know that even as a nurse I hate taking medicine and especially going into hospitals. So, on the day I voluntarily do either I *have* to be really sick.

After I couldn't stand it any longer I finally went to see a specialist. Following a battery of tests, I was finally diagnosed with the condition called achalasia. Achalasia is a rare condition characterized by a loss of esophageal motility. The condition affects one in one hundred thousand people. The difficulty is that the muscle of the esophagus just above the stomach tightens like a rubber band and won't allow food to pass into the stomach. The food that is supposed to go down into your stomach cannot pass, so it collects in your esophagus causing food to just sit in your chest. *YUCK!* What an awful feeling. After a while you can only hold so much food content in your chest so what can't go down must come up. Imagine living your life like that *day after day after day*, not being able to swallow. By the time I got to a Doctor I weighted only ninety-nine pounds.

Now I know why they call it a battery of tests because after they get done poking pipes down my throat it soon feels like you swallowed a small car battery. Did I forget to tell you that you will need humor to get you through this maze? Honey, I had to find reasons to laugh just to keep from crying.

Now that I knew what I was dealing with I began the treatment for achalasia. Since this was a mechanical issue we called in an esophageal mechanic better known as a surgeon. The surgeon performed a procedure on me called an esophageal Myotomy. It left me with a tribal marking scar from my back to my chest for life. Here's what happens during this lovely procedure. They pull out my esophagus and cut the outer muscle to allow the tightness of the inner muscle to relax. The doctor says to me, "This may only last for one year." Remind me to write a book on the power of suggestion. One year to the day I was choking again.

Struggling to eat—now every day—I was trying to swallow food. Some days I could and many days I couldn't. I tried to ignore it all, but you can only ignore dying of starvation for so long. It was impacting every area of my life. I began looking emaciated at five feet six inches and just at 100 pounds. I wanted to shout to the world, *"I AM NOT ANOREXIC! NO, I'M NOT BULIMIC! SO, STOP LOOKING AT ME LIKE THAT!"*

This situation affected me emotionally. As I became increasingly discouraged I thought to myself that I would never be normal again. It impacted me spiritually when I had those moments when I thought, "How could the God that I love and serve allow me to suffer like this? I will explore this more in the spiritual maze."

Giving Birth in the Health Maze

I don't know if any of us will ever really understand the sovereignty of God. Maybe one

day we can sit down with him and get all our
unanswered questions answered. His
sovereignty however means that he can do
things however he wants to do it, and use any
situation to bring us into that reality and our
destiny.

The *last* thing I was thinking about
during the peak of my illness was giving birth.
Yet God had another plan. It *would* be right in
the midst of my illness that I would give birth to
two beautiful children. I even gave birth to the
vision for my life.

Both of my pregnancies were traumatic.
A pregnancy in itself is an issue. Try adding an
additional physical illness to that. Of course,

you could imagine it made carrying and birth a challenge. Despite the difficulty I was still having with my esophagus, somehow, I managed to bring two healthy girls into the world.

And if that wasn't enough, I guess the Doctors failed to see there was a third baby on board. It wasn't a boy or a girl, but it was my vision. Please hear me when I say that the enemy has no power to stop the plan of God. As sick as I was I still carried the vision God placed in my heart and then gave birth to it.

Despite my continued illness I worked every day as a Nurse. Nursing would pay the bills; however, it left much to be desired in the area of creativity. To try to meet my need for creativity I'd do just about anything at work. I laugh now when I think about volunteering at work to put up an educational Bulletin board, just so I could satisfy my creative appetite. The Board was a colorful creative board about Colostomy's. You never knew how creative Bowel education could be. *Lordy, Lordy,* I reckon I was really grasping at straws to feed that need for creativity in my life.

Somehow—in all of God's sovereignty—He allowed the birthing of the vision that would meet my creative desires as well as create a way for him to get the Glory. I would later come to find out that the births of my daughters were also part of the strategic plan of God for the vison.

The vision would be called KIDDS Dance project, a nonprofit organization for youth that builds character in youth through the performing arts. My oldest daughter would grow up to become the Choreographer and my youngest daughter would become the Music Director. Then God loved me enough to also provide me another person who is much like a third daughter to me that became my Stage Manager.

I have said on numerous occasions, it is no coincidence that God would call me to be a Writer and Director only to give me a

Choreographer, Music Director and a Stage Manager as daughters. If He was that intentional about those things then He was probably that intentional about my illness. That would mean that even in my illness there is a Purpose.

If not but for to only let somebody else know they can live with and through an illness then that was and still is the purpose. It could also have been for letting other people with the diagnosis of Achalasia know that they are not alone. Knowing the fact that this condition only affects one in 100,000 people, I decided to stop thinking how awful I am and started thinking I must be very special to God. There must be

some strategic and divine reason I was chosen to
go through this.

Over the years I would be treated by
several different Doctors. I've witnessed
multiple Doctors try their best to stay abreast of
the latest news regarding my case. I once even
had a Doctor allow me to do self-dilatations of
my own esophagus at home. I know that sounds
bizarre. He ordered me a two-foot-long tapered
rubber tubing that I would jam down my own
throat periodically to stretch that muscle
whenever that muscle would get too tight to
swallow. Now for those of you who are saying
how in the world could you do that to yourself I
say this. It's the same concept as a diabetic

having to inject themselves with insulin daily. If you know your life depends on it you will do whatever it takes to live.

The wonders of modern medicine are constantly changing and improving the treatment of many illnesses. However, people who are ill just pray that they live long enough to see the cure. Remember when the HIV & AIDS Virus used to be a death sentence, but now modern medicine can treat the virus to the point of almost nonexistence. The same is happening with the condition of Achalasia. During an interim when my current Doctor was nowhere to be found, I was forced to seek out a new Doctor. Oh Lord, here we go; another major turn in the Health Maze. Finding this new Doctor also led me to the knowledge of a new treatment available for patients suffering with Achalasia. Remember? God always has a plan because He's sovereign. The treatment was a laparoscopic surgical procedure called a POEM (per-oral endoscopic exam).

I don't want to turn this into a medical journal so let me explain this in lay terms. The word Laparoscopic simply means that instead of making big incisions in my chest they could now just pass a tube down my throat and make a small incision on the inside to relieve the tightness in my esophagus. The benefits would be amazing. No outer scars, no long hospital stay and a quick return to work.

Not only had I found the best procedure but I happen to find one of the leading Doctors in the country to perform it. What are the odds of that? I was told that there were only five surgeons in U.S. that could even perform this procedure, and two of them practiced right here in Atlanta. Wow, how fortunate for me!

During this time, I found myself in the hospital once again after a prolonged three weeks without food. My poor children insisted I go into the hospital. I don't even know how I was still walking around. It would be a long five days in the hospital. I was being fed intravenously because I still could not swallow.

Just before I was admitted; however, I researched the Doctor who I found to be one of the two physicians that could perform the POEM procedure. I can remember being in the hospital Emergency Room when I introduced myself to him in an email. He actually emailed me back stating he could help me. What a relief I felt just at the thought that someone could make me better. While there each day I kept trying to get a message to him. I wanted to keep in touch. I was calling his office every day from my hospital bed. I was right on the verge of pulling that hospital gown together in the back to cover my pride and rolling my IV pole right across the street and just stand outside of his office until I could get his attention. Thank God, I had not quite lost my good common sense yet. Nevertheless, you do know that desperate times call for desperate measures.

I can remember standing at the window of my hospital room and looking at this huge crane just outside the window. My thought was, "If only I could get on the top of that crane." I could see myself waving a sign with the Doctors name on it. I was *so* desperate for help. Perhaps that would finally get his attention. On day five after almost giving up hope suddenly, I looked up and that Doctor who I so desperately wanted to see finally walked into my room. He was a man of short stature and powerful wisdom like the Apostle Paul. He was of Asian descent. A man of few words but he got right to the point. He knew exactly what I wanted and needed. He cut out and surpassed any extraneous additional testing anybody else had planned and told me he would help me. In the interim, he allowed me to be discharged and then had me to return for a treatment of Botox injection therapy to tide me over until I could get scheduled for the POEM surgery.

Let me say right here—regarding Botox—most people who hear that word only know Botox either as a cosmetic beautification procedure or a deadly poison. The truth of the matter is it's both. However, in my case Botox was one of the temporary treatments for Achalasia. Botox comes from a deadly bacterium but when used in small doses in a controlled environment can make a world of difference when it comes to being able to swallow. We've all heard the phrase, "What doesn't kill you makes you stronger." Well the use of Botox is a literal demonstration of that truth for me.

Let's all take a moment to gain a little strength right here in the midst this knowledge. The enemy has sent many things our way to try to take us all out. This Health Maze can be tricky. However, God knows just how much we can bear. He is the great physician and knows just how much of a painful experience we can tolerate. He won't let the enemy take us out. With God on our side the thing the enemy sent to kill us will now make us stronger. In my case, it was this medicine. The physician God sent my way was ready, willing, and able to give me the help I needed. I was so ecstatic about my coming new-found ability to eat that I started making celebration plans. I even jumped the gun a little and wrote a poem for my doctor in exchange for the P.O.E.M. surgery that my Doctor was about to perform on me.

I had the poem printed on special paper and had it specially framed. Look at me. There goes my creative side again. I hand delivered the poem to his office one day long before my surgery. What could stop me now? It read:

The P.O.E.M.

Physician of Extraordinary Mastery

It's often been said

In this life we've begun

There are Jacks of all trades

And Masters of none

Yet I recently found

The latter not true

There's a Master of all

I'll share him with you

He's a Master of knowledge

In the great G.I. field

Understanding the complex

He believes you can heal

He's a Master of kindness

With a warm heart he greats

Never too busy

To bless those he meets

He's a Master of Sacrifice

Finding time when there's none

To see one more person

Even after he's done

God truly has given

This gift that you do

It's time for a poem

To be given to you

Think Like David

So, there I was, ready or not here I come. I was ready and the Doctor was ready but there was just one last thing. I was standing in the middle of the Health Maze with a great big giant wall standing in between us. The wall was invisible and on the day we finally met, neither of us could see it.

When the wall finally manifested itself, I tried everything in my power to overcome it. I tried climbing over it. I tried to circumvent it. I even tried going through it but the wall would turn out to be impenetrable. The name of that wall would be called Insurance Pre-certification. That's the approval you get from the Insurance Company before they agree to pay for your surgery. What normal human being would deny another human being the right to swallow food?

The denial letter I would receive spoke those inhumane words verbatim. "We cannot approve the surgery to help you to swallow." *ARE YOU INSANE?* Do you even hear yourself talking? Most of you can't even stand to miss lunch and here they are expecting me to live for days upon days without eating. How dare they! *HOW DARE THEY!* My Life is at stake!

I guess those inflammatory remarks could be considered as excerpts from my response letters and there would be many to come. They just opened the door to a game that I play well. It's the writing game. I didn't think I could win but one thing I knew for sure, I knew I could at least play the writing game long enough to annoy them.

LET THE GAMES BEGIN! Now no one in their right mind thinks they really have the power to stand up against a Giant. This was no mom and pop shop. It was now me against a major *billion*-dollar Insurance Corporation. At

Church, we always heard we should dance like David danced but now I had to begin to start *thinking* like David thought.

Let's look at this for a moment. David had no fear of Goliath. The giant's size and his banter did not matter to the little shepherd boy. David recalled having to fight some other battles in his past and he remembered how he won some impossible battles before then. Those same battles gave him the confidence to go forth into battle with Goliath. Listen, I don't know what battle you may be facing right now, but you must remember that God has already brought you through some previous battles. The old song writer said, "Through many dangers toils and snares I have already come, tis grace hath brought me safe thus far and grace shall lead me home. God's grace is sufficient for you even now."

So, I remember one of the Doctors telling his Colleagues one day that this patient *(referring to me)* was very astute about her condition. You can bet that I had studied and researched every possible thing that I could about the condition. I felt that I knew every conventional and unconventional treatment that existed. My urge to gain that knowledge would prove to be very beneficial for the literary battle I was about to enter.

The argument of the Insurance Company was that the procedure was experimental and there were not enough studies to prove its efficacy. My research proved without a doubt that the surgery had been done countless times and I pulled case after case showing that 95% of the patients having had the procedure were much improved. I even researched to the point that I dispelled the fact given to me that there were only five Physicians in the states who could do the procedure. Although the procedure was discovered by a physician in China, I discovered evidence and a chart listing *multiple* physicians all over the United States that were performing the procedure with marked success.

At one point during the back and forth letters between the Company and myself they actually cancelled my Insurance. I was not the least bit phased and I continued to write even more fervently than ever. I was like David except I didn't have a stone, but I had a small ink pen in my pocket at all times. I must give credit to the old Englishman Edward Bulwer-Lytton who first penned the words, "the Pen is Mightier than the sword." His great wisdom was in action at this point.

Speaking with other health care staff I found out it was a commonality for people to be denied the procedure. I found out I was not the only person fighting this same battle for life.

This new-found information fueled my fury to gain a justice for others. I was still stuck in the Maze of Health, but a light must have been shinning down from heaven because I could see clearly the direction to take next. My next move was to take my writing to the next level.

I remembered that I just happen to have a friend who was a Legislative Representative. So, I sat down one day and wrote her my story. At this point I realized that this battle was not just about me but I was now fighting for every patient with Achalasia who had been denied the right to swallow. Immediately upon her receipt of my information she gave me direction for how to properly go about having this addressed in the Legislature. I would now have to write my own bill. And so, I did. I wrote *The Achalasia Bill*.

In my notification to the Insurance Company of my continued pursuit for justice someone in the company grew tired of my antics and without my requesting it, they renewed my Insurance coverage. *YAAAAY ME!* But this battle was *far* from over honey. The Bill was surpassed by other issues that deemed more important on the Legislative table the first go around so it will take a continued effort to try to get the bill passed.

I at least enjoyed the thought that the letters did get some attention, and I did not just take it lying down. I can also say that I'm proud that I learned how to write and submit a bill. God is bigger than all the giants in our lives and with God we will win in the end.

Pain Is a Propeller

As uncomfortable as pain and painful situations can be in our lives remember nothing can happen except God allow it. Pain can be a tremendous propeller to advance us through the mazes of life, and to move us closer to our destinations.

I just heard the story of a woman who had to drop out of school due to unbearable migraine headaches. While sitting home killing time; however, she could clearly hear God leading her to start an organization to help the homeless. Her organization has since been a tremendous success.

The Father has clearly spoken to each of us regarding our pains. His word says, "In everything give thanks for this is the will of God in Christ Jesus concerning you *(1 Thessalonians 5:18).*" We can look at our pain and truly be thankful knowing that God has the power of our pain in his hand and in it there is purpose.

"They overcame by the blood of the lamb and the words of their testimony..."

- *Revelation 12:11*

2

The Wealth Maze

I was walking out of a restaurant one night, and I noticed that the car parked at the door had a magnetic sign stuck on the side of it. The sign was an ad for the business that the driver conducted. As I walked away I had a thought. My thought was that I would like to amass an amount of money that would make it inappropriate for me to place magnetic signs on my car to advertise what I do.

As I walked on, I thought to myself, "I want to drive the kind of car that would be inappropriate to actually stick signs on it." I mean, really, when is the last time you saw a Bentley with a sticker saying, "My child made honor roll," or a Rolls Royce with that silhouette sticker of the family of four with the dog? Lol. I once had a conversation with a coworker and we agreed that it would be cool to have a job where nobody really knew what you did except you. All they'd know is that you get paid well for doing what you do.

College Days

Every parent wants to see their child grow up to be successful. That image of success would involve them being able to financially care for themselves. One way to do that would be to get a lucrative secure career. Right? My heart was always interested in the performing arts, but my father would insist that I choose a more stable and traditional career. It was his desire that I become a Pharmacist like his good friend. I looked at that vision for a moment and saw myself getting really bored living a life of counting pills. I also feared that the artist in me might begin color coding the pills and delivering them per color and not per prescription. That would not be good. So, the next best thing for me was Nursing. I love people and I thought that white uniform with the matching cap was cool at the time. I'm also into fashion so the outfit won me over. Off I went to Florida A&M University, and four years later I held a BS Degree in Nursing. I was ready to treat patients and make money so I could be financially stable, right? Wrong! What Nurse is unemployed? What person would have a college degree and can't get a job? It is so unfortunate, but this scenario happens every day. What a disheartening matter, or should I say another maze.

Let the Wealth Maze Begin!

Right after graduating from college I was about to enter the Wealth Maze and traveling blindly for the next couple of *years*. What happened? I'm glad you asked. Well unfortunately it is not enough just to endure four years of college and get the nursing degree. After that you must then pass the State Board Exam! Six times I failed the Nursing Board and the exam is only given every six months. What a Maze. I meant what an *amazing* ride! I tried and I cried. I tried again and I cried again. *Six times!* Can you believe it? Why did I even keep trying? In the meantime, I would work as a nursing assistant. I recall feeling demeaned while working in this position. One day I crossed paths with a person I had graduated with who passed her Boards right away. I will never forget that sinking feeling I had in my gut when she began to share with me all the things she was able to purchase—including a home—just because she passed the exam and got the *real* RN Nursing job. *Ugggh!* I felt awful. When I got to myself, honey I cried again.

Going from one nurse aide job to another I ended up at a place called *The Jewish Home*. It was a nursing facility with a Director whom God had strategically placed in my Wealth Maze for an appointed time. I can still remember the day she called me into her office. I worked at the facility long before she got hired so there was no reason for her to pull my file. I knew I had not done anything wrong. I was a model employee I'm told. Lol. I was always on time. I got along with every employee, even the difficult ones. I gave excellent patient care because I love people. I even went beyond the call of duty, singing for patients and painting their nails. I became like the Apostle Paul and I was *wherewith content.* But the Director found out something about me.

Looking through my file she discovered that I had a BS degree in Nursing. When she asked why I was working as a nurse's aide I had to tell her where I was in the maze of life. That moment was the beginning of our love-hate relationship. I loved her for taking an interest in helping me get out of the rat race, and I hated her because she was *relentless* and would not let me stay at the place where I was. Lol.

What supervisor goes to an employee's home to harass them? One day, this woman actually came to my house! She picked me up and physically took me to the Greyhound Bus station. She literally *made* me go back to Jacksonville, Florida to take that Nursing Board exam *AGAIN! Why Lord! WHY?* I just couldn't! I couldn't keep putting myself through that kind of emotional turmoil. Why would she not just leave me alone? But she would not let it go because she saw something in me. *THANK YOU, JESUS, FOR MS. JEAN!* I conceded to her badgering and went back to Jacksonville. I still remember sitting there doodling as they gave out the routine directions. I had memorized the directions at this point. I can clearly remember having an *"I don't care"* attitude. I had to do that to try to protect myself from the impending pain. It didn't matter how many times I took the test, it still hurt every time I got that Failure Letter.

I'm in tears even now as I write these words. As I think about it, it's now over thirty years later. How in the world can I still feel how painful that was? I know exactly why. As a nurse, I have dealt with people who have overdosed or ingested poison. According to the poison control center the usual treatment is to give the patient meds to cause them to regurgitate and rid the body of the poison. This is the treatment approach for most poisons except for something like bleach. In a severe case such as bleach, the theory is to never cause the patient to regurgitate because if it burned going down it will burn again coming up. And that's just what happened to me. It's the reason many people bury feelings of hurt and pain for years. They do so just to avoid feeling that burn twice. I was just going through the motions.

Try Again

I returned to Atlanta hoping she was happy that I at least did it. Then the routine painful waiting process began. Weeks went by and I was settled back in my routine and quite content. Then I came home one day and there it was *the letter*. I saw it lying on the dining room

table where I later discovered my husband had
strategically placed it for me to find. I walked
passed it with no desire to open it. I had no
interest in opening that deep wound again. I had
so conveniently covered it so well. I was good
at pretending it didn't matter. When my
husband saw that I was avoiding the letter like
the plague he lovingly pushed me down on the
sofa and lay on top of me. Then he began to
read the letter out loud. As soon as I heard the
word *PASSED,* I nearly passed out! I couldn't
believe it. My husband is a clown and I loved
him for his sense of humor, but as silly as he can
be even he would not do something that cruel.
He wouldn't joke about this matter. It was too
close to my heart. I took the letter and had to

read it for myself. It was true. *I PASSED! I PASSED!* Did you hear me I said *I PASSED!*

My Director and I both soon left The Jewish Home and went to open a New Luxury High Rise Facility in the heart of Buckhead. That's where the wealthy live for you out of towners. My Boss became the Director and I became the Assistant Director. Look at God!

Again, I hear God speaking clearly to you through my words. He's saying to you, "For I know the plans I have for you; plans to prosper you and not to harm you." God does not gain any joy from our pain, and He insists on getting the glory. Whatever happened to you in the past--*YES* whatever it was--it *HAD TO HAPPEN.*

When Mary and Martha were distraught over their brother Lazarus being ill they sent someone to go tell Jesus he was needed. Instead of Jesus coming he sent the messenger back to tell them, "This sickness was not unto death but for the Glory of God." The Bible never mentioned the messengers name nor if it was a man, woman, or a child. But what I do know is that God is still using messengers today to remind people—who are experiencing tremendous pain—that He *WILL* get the Glory out of your life. I'm your messenger today. And I'm speaking loud and clear. The reason you're at this point in the Wealth Maze right now is because you're supposed to be. God's strategically ordering your steps. Soon you will be in the right place at the right time if you don't faint or give up. Be attentive and listen. God's sending messengers with messages your way. I'm one of them.

And so, I progressed through the Wealth Maze. From that day forward I never had a nursing job that I did not get an immediate promotion to management. More Management, More Money! I eventually bought that beautiful home I so desired!

Even now, I now see God moving me into an even greater wealth dimension as a

Pastor, Speaker, Author and Playwright. He is about to get the glory from everything that has happened in my life and I am about to get paid what I am worth. It's all working. You just have to speak it into existence. I'm no stranger to speaking things into existence.

Know Your Worth

And while we're talking about worth, let's talk about yours. God has given you many gifts, skills, and talents. You probably recall his words that say, "He has given you the power to get wealth." I know if you really stop to think about it, you can think of many gifts that you have and they can be monetized. I have a word for those of you who feel you cannot ask for money for what you do or always under estimate your worth. After all I am a voice crying out in the Wealth Maze right now. The word that gave me financial freedom is what I will share with you right now. "If people paid you what you are really worth, it would put you in a position to bless many more people. Stop thinking it's all about you. If you think what you do is for the people then you're right it is. So, the next time you get ready to do those things you know God called and skilled you to do, do it with others in mind and it will boost your confidence so say, "It's not free." Here's another piece of advice. "Get a vision board. If you already have one, go back and review your vision board. Did your board become static?

Are there still things on your board you thought you would have done by now but don't see the manifestation and reality of it at all? You may want to try something I recently did. Long term goals are great, but I decided to do a board of short term goals. I created a flyer advertising everything I will be doing this year. Key words are *THIS YEAR.* Live on Purpose and do something every day that's moving towards your goal. Reevaluate each project at the end of twelve months. If it didn't happen reevaluate it. But if it did happen then it will give you that psychological boost to know that, 'You can do all things through Christ.'"

There is one other gift I would like to discuss while we are still talking about the Wealth Maze. Understand that there are many ways to attain wealth. You can work hard for it or you can ask for it. Now isn't that a novel idea? Imagine that, just the thought of simply asking people for money. Most of us have had a day and time that we might have had to ask a friend for a dollar. Right? A dollar is one thing between friends, but what if you have a vision that needs thousands of dollars. How do you fund the vision? Well, at some point during my journey towards wealth I learned the art of Grant Writing. *WHOA!* Where had this secret been all my life? Lol. You mean you can just ask somebody for money, not have to work for

it and not have to pay it back? Yep! Sure can.
(I'm aware this is not proper English, but it just helps to get the message across. Lol.) Anyhow, that's exactly what I did.

Another Turn in the Maze

It started when I decided that I could not let go of my love for the performing arts. Of course, Nursing had proven itself to be lucrative, but money will never take the place of passion. That's one lesson you need to learn now while you're going down the paths and corridors of this Wealth Maze. A Prophet came to my home one day and said to me, "Do what you love and the money will follow." My love for the Arts pushed me to start a nonprofit

organization called *KIDDS Dance Project*.
Now this is a story of real irony.

I loved the Arts because I could sing.
Sometimes I imagined what it would be like to
be an opera singer. As a child, I remember
standing in my living room practicing every
song from *The Sound of Music* with hopes of
seeing Broadway someday. Now the singing
was fine, but then God led me to start a dance
program. *DANCE?* I'm not a dancer. I began
to sound a little bit like Moses who tried to
convince God to choose his brother as the
speaker instead of him. "Why me God?" I
quickly learned the answer to that. If God sent a
professional dancer to do the assignment they

might have said how good they are as people
applauded the productions. But having no
dance training at all, I was forced to give God
all the glory. I knew it was no way I could do
these professional stage productions that I do
now without the anointing of God. God had
some pretty big requests and he financed every
bit of it. The organization only performs on the
major stages of the city and even performed on
New York City Off-Broadway.

Here's the next key word on this
journey: *professional.* It didn't take long to
learn that these professional stages cost
thousands of dollars to house the productions
God was putting in my head. I'm glad these

were his ideals. This meant He had to pay for them. And honey, He had a plan.

A parent of one of the children I used to work with was a Grant Writer for the state of Georgia. When she saw me struggling to get money to fund the vision she simply said to me, "You should write grants." Mind you that was all the information I got. There was no grant writing class like I now do for others, but her statement that day turned a light bulb on in my head. I began to read, research, and write, and write and write and before you knew it I had written over $250,000 worth of grants for my nonprofit. My new philosophy was, " I ain't washing no cars and I ain't baking no cookies to fund my shows.

And if I bake a cookie, I'm only going to bake just one and sell it in a silent auction for $20,000." And yes, I say it in that vernacular.

If you ever heard the statement, "You can't take it with you," well it's true. Do you know how many people die every day and leave money on this earth with no children to inherit it? That's just a reference to money from those gone on, but the bulk of the funding I get is from Foundations and Corporations that are very much alive. I think I'm going to start something in this book called *Patisms*. It's going to be the philosophies that I've learned and exercised based on my own experiences.

Patism #1:

"Favor is the distance between your present state and your success."

One Corporation gave me $50,000 to fund the vision God gave me for the kids. Now this story has not ended just yet, but let me at least get you started. When the money came I was ecstatic to say the least. I would be remiss not to mention the fact that an act of favor is what really put me in the front of the line to receive the grant. People from all over the United States had to vote for their favorite nonprofit. Little did I know that there was a woman with her own nonprofit in another state watching my progress online. During the progression of the grant I received a phone call out of the blue from that woman whom I had never met in my life. She explained to me how she had been watching me and wanted to help me get the grant. She decided to have all 4000 members of her organization to vote for my organization every day until the voting was over. That kind of favor gave me the edge I needed to win the grant. A new building was now being built for us and it would take six months for it to be constructed. I took a team of people out and we signed up three hundred new kids for our program in one day.

We held on to the three hundred names feeling we had a sufficient clientele of children and parents to sustain the program. When the building was finished I had to pinch myself to see if this was real. One day while I was alone in the new *KIDDS Center* I fell on my face and praised God like never before for giving me the desires of my heart. I'm telling you this was a dream come true. This facility had everything I could imagine I wanted for the kids. I wanted it to be the kind of place where kids would not even want to ever leave. My inspiration for the facility came from my visit in a juvenile detention center.

From time to time I am called upon to intervene when a child's behavior becomes challenging at home. A parent subsequently had asked me to visit their son who had been incarcerated. When I went to see him, I was escorted through a facility where I saw young black males seemingly enjoying life. They were just having a ball playing basketball, ping pong and watching their favorite TV shows. The moment I saw this, the light came on *DING!* Why did we as a community have to wait until these boys got behind locked doors to offer them these recreational opportunities? From then on, I was on a mission.

Our facility had basketball, air hockey, ping pong, a pool table, electric basketball, seven keyboards for a music class, our own private auditorium for performances, and a 4500-sq. ft. dance studio. What more could we ask for? Right? Then the day had come for us to notify the three hundred students we signed up for the program about the facility. Only ten of them appeared. For weeks and weeks, we struggled to maintain and keep the doors open. The minimal enrollment was simply not enough to sustain us. This was supposed to turn out to be one of my streams of income. I found myself working day and night. I worked twelve hour days at the facility taking just a stipend *(far from a salary)* to make sure we had lights. I can truly say that it was the best of times, and it was the absolute worse. There I was, living amid my lifelong dream and miserable. What an oxymoron. I'm in the midst of the Wealth Maze and cannot find my way out. I thought I had hit jackpot, but it only turned out to be another empty dark room in the Wealth Maze, and I felt this time I was trapped with no door openings to let me out. It was a slow painful death of a dream. At first, we decided just to shut down one half of the building. The bills were mounting and we were going under like quicksand. I held on as long as I could. I felt like I was holding on to someone the Doctors had long pronounced as dead, but every now and then the dream would gasp for breath making me feel like it could live again. "Let it go Pat," are the words I kept hearing. It was just too hard to hear those words but the moment came when I conceded.

I can still see myself in that meeting. The discussion was about clearing out of the building and deciding which items we should take with us. My hurt and pain had turned into anger. I sat there in tears saying, "I DON'T WANT ANY OF IT!" It was probably the second most painful moment of my life. Your dreams are attached to your very soul. So, to have that taken away is just beyond what I can explain. My greatest fear in life is not death, but life without being able to live my dream.

"Where there is no vision the people perish"

-   *Proverbs 29:18*

I gave *it* all up. I gave the building and belongings up, but I never gave up my dream. Dreams are immortal and nothing on earth can really kill a dream. It will live on through all eternity. To this day I still hold on to the hope that the *KIDDS Center* will exist again.

You know, God is certainly a jealous God. In retrospect, I know that it took the support of many people across these United States as well as people right in my circle to help this grant award come to pass. But I also remember a moment when someone—involved with the project—basked in the glory of how *they* made it happen. I am openly confessing in this book that I feel it in my gut that God was not pleased with this. Whatever happened God had to get all the glory. I was happy with the funding and celebrated the project, but the thought that I would give someone else even a portion of his glory was nagging at my inner most being. Even when we have the knowledge, the wherewithal, the skills, the relationships and the resources to get a job done we still have to acknowledge God as the giver of all gifts. It takes a tremendous amount of humility to get in that place. But you'll learn this as you mosey on down the paths of the Wealth Maze.

Now that I had practically lost $50,000 what would I do next? You can't imagine how many times I have said to myself, "How in the world could I ever get that kind of funding again?" Who else is going to gift me that kind of money? Then I remembered that the God I serve has endless resources.

That would mean not only can God redistribute $50,000, but he actually has the resources to double and triple that. In fact, God made a specific statement regarding his method of blessing us. His word says, *"Now unto him who is able to do exceeding, abundantly above all that we ask or think according to the power that worketh in us (Ephesians 3:20)."* For that reason, my dream still lives on and those very words gave me the intestinal fortitude to do what I did next. I found a foundation that started its organization with a mere six million dollars. I know, right? Lol. Yes, I am saying that sarcastically. Today that same foundation holds six hundred and ten million dollars in assets. Knowing this, I figured it would be ok to put my request in before the Board. And so, I did. I wrote a proposal and asked them for $1.5 million dollars. My heavenly Father also says, "You have not because you ask not," so I asked. What do I have to lose? They will either say yes or no. Why would they want to let the money just sit and constantly collect interest? All I need is the Favor of God and to have just one person in that board room give me a chance to prove myself. This same foundation stated that they like to do site visits. I thought, Man! If they came out to physically see what I do with the children then *GAME OVER*!" This of course is a story and a work still in progress, but believe me I will let the world know the outcome. Either way you can know right now that Pat Martin is never going to give up on her dream. I will continue to wander and make my way through this Wealth Maze until God shows me the opening. He's done it once on a $50,000 level. What makes you think He won't do it again? It's just a matter of time. One thing you've got to have while walking the course is determination.

Patism #2:

"If poverty is a mindset before it's a reality then so is wealth."

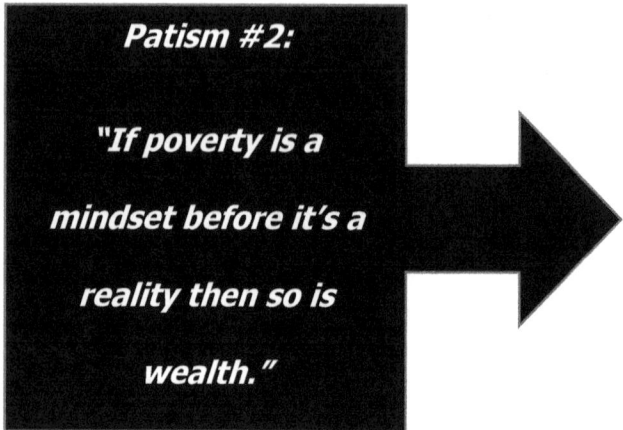

Many times, we find ourselves in the midst of situations, and feel we have no power over them. Although we may not be able to change the situation we surely do have the power to change our perspective about the situation. An occurrence that may seem like a bad thing could turn out to be the best thing that ever happened to you. This is if you're looking at the grand scheme of things.

Elevate Your Mind

"For as he thinketh in his heart so is he"

- *Proverbs 23:7*

We must elevate our thinking to the point where we can overcome negative defeating thoughts with the power of positive thoughts. There's one strategy that will begin disconnecting you from your negative disconcerting thoughts and people, and that is connecting yourself with positive people with positive thoughts. This may seem trivial. But all you need is a little bit. Even if it's a little bit of faith.

Patism #3:

"All you have is all you need."

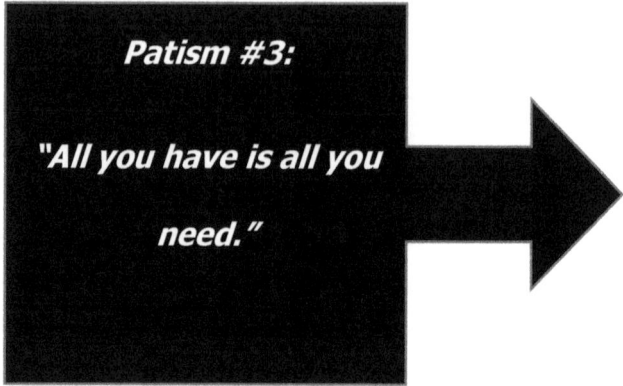

Our immediate resources may seem limited; however, little is much in the hands of God. Another strategy is to begin visualizing yourself as successful. Visualize yourself having more than enough. Be willing to allow God to use you and whatever resources you do have available. God will supernaturally make the difference.

The day I thought about taking the kids that I still have in my nonprofit to New York I only had $100 in my bank account. But my money did not keep me from visualizing the dream. I saw the kids and I standing on that Off-Broadway stage. That visualization somehow eventually manifested itself and turned into a reality. So that $100 I started with soon turned into $30,000.

The Alchemist taught me a very valuable principle in life. The theory is that if you just start doing something you really want then the Universe will give you everything you need to do it. I have written a stage play called *The Butterfly*. Having now studied a lot of the butterfly behaviors there are two behaviors it possesses that give it power. First, the butterfly does not speak. Have you ever heard the butterfly make a sound? No, and you never will. For whatever reason, when God created them he made them incapable of making sound. That's powerful, especially considering it flies by the flapping of its wings. Nevertheless, the butterfly makes no sound at all. Oh, what about this? Did you know that when a butterfly flaps its wings it creates a momentum in the atmosphere that has the capability to create a tsunami storm on the other side of the world? Those combined behaviors say to me that even if I am not a big talker, my actions towards the vision will speak much louder than what I say.

Stop telling people what you're going to do and just do it! I've learned this lesson on the Wealth Maze. There will be many who don't believe you. There will be others who don't want you to do it for whatever reason. You'll learn to stop talking and telling people everything on this journey.

There's another creature that drives the point home of "all you need is a little bit." That creature is the bumblebee. Most of us have heard that it is not scientifically possible for a bumblebee to fly, but they go right on flying, don't they? It's probably not financially or physically possible for you to do the things that God is about to have you do? But guess what?

It's about to happen. And when it does happen, people will look at you and wonder how you did it. You can look at them and say, "I trusted God with my limited resources and it happened. I used my little bit and had faith that it would make a big impact. See, small faith in a *BIG* God can make a world of difference."

Many people probably spend a lifetime trying to maneuver their way through this Wealth Maze. But one good thing to know is that there is more than one way to the prize. God can create a door where no door even existed. That's the wonder of our God. That means if you find yourself in a place where you are unemployed, God can help you create a job

out of nothing. If you find yourself at a dead
end with the job or career you do have, God
knows how to give you creative insight and
wisdom on how to turn the corner. If God could
make all mankind out of dirt then what more
can he do creatively with you? Remember he *is*
the great creator?

Resourcefulness Breeds Success

The way things work in my Wealth
Maze is based on the theory of need. My family
members may say I'm a cheapskate. When I
was younger I went grocery shopping with my
younger sister. She would always buy things in
bulk and this particular day we both wanted to
buy some jelly. Both of us had very little funds,

and that thought always mandated my spending habits. So as usual she bought the huge family jar of jelly, and I bought the smallest one I could find so I could get change back. On the way home when it was time to get back on the train her money was short and she asked me if she could borrow change for the train. I jokingly told her she better put some of that jelly in the payment stall. I was proud of the fact that I had plenty of money left over. Even to this day I own a name brand purse only because it was a Mother's Day gift from my daughters. My philosophy is I never want to have a bag whose value is higher than what is in my wallet that it holds. Now being too frugal with money is not really a good thing; however, I have seen people reap the benefits of my frugality.

Your ability to maneuver through the Wealth Maze will depend a lot on your own ingenuity. How resourceful are you with the things you already have? All you have is all you really need. If you plant the seed in your hand you will soon have an entire orchard. You have far more than you think you have.

3

The Relationship Maze

Six feet two light skinned with long hair was the order I placed. I couldn't have asked for a better selection. It was as if I had been given a menu to order a man for my life, and I got exactly what I asked for. Therein lay the danger. Sometimes you get exactly what you asked for. The only issue is that we often ask for what we want, and not for what we need.

It's hard to ask for what you need when you're still trying to just figure out who you are.

There ought to be some kind of rule. The rule should say, "You cannot connect yourself to anybody until after you know who you are and what your needs are." I believe we act as if we're puzzle pieces. When we want to win badly we simply just force the pieces to fit. We don't really care whether they fit or not.

I was no different than the next girl. I loved the attention any boy would give me, and one day I got that attention from someone that I assumed to be *the one*. Question is, "Was he?" I often remind people that every time God created something on Earth He'd step back and say, "It was good." But there's one thing God saw and knew it was not good. For God, it was not good for man to be alone. Our innate desire for love and companionship stems from God's desire for us to have it. Although connecting with others can be a task in itself. The even greater task is finding the right one.

In our natural physical state, we are often driven through the Maze of Relationships by our eyes. We want what looks good. A good look alone; however, can be as tempting as a sugar-coated dessert but just as detrimental to our emotional and physical health. It is ironic that marriage would be referred to as an institution. That almost sounds like one would have to be downright silly or even a little insane to attach themselves to one person for the rest of their lives. Is it an institution of an imprisonment nature? Is marriage an unnatural institution that holds us hostage against one's will, keeping one from exploring his or her own life path and destiny? Or is it an institution of education, a place of Higher Learning? Do we learn mysteries about life, ourselves, and our path as we embark upon a journey of living together with the one we love? If we are to learn these things, then how and when will the lessons manifest themselves?

You see there are several junctures, boundaries, and phases in the Relationship Maze. This particular maze is multi-faceted and multi-leveled. As you journey through your

human life you are sure to experience
relationships of all kinds and sorts, and on many
different levels. Some examples of the
relationship phases (in no particular order) are:

- *The Womb Relationship – between a mother and baby*
- *The Baby Bonding Relationship – between baby, parents, and other close relatives*
- *The Sibling Relationship – between child and siblings*
- *The Education Relationship – between child and teacher*

- *The Boyfriend/Girlfriend Relationship – between person and usually the opposite sex*
- *The Faith Relationship – between person and Higher Being (God)*
- *The Money Relationship – between person and their money*
- *The Job Relationships-*
  - *Between person and manager*
  - *Between person and client, etc.*
- *The Marriage Relationship – between person and spouse*

- o *The Have and to Hold Stage*
- o *The for Better or Worse Stage*
- o *For Richer or Poor Stage*
- o *Til Death Do Us Part Stage*

While it's possible to elaborate on these types of relationships and more, let's focus on The Marriage Relationship for a moment. I will elaborate on the other types of relationships I've experienced perhaps in another book. Nonetheless, The Marriage Relationship juncture is what I would like to highlight as it pertains to my life.

To Have and to Hold Stage

"To hold me is to have me"

Now, the more I look at those words I'm just coming into the realization that *to hold me* is *to have me*. Not in a bondage or imprisonment kind of way, but in a loving way. I've come to the revelation that to hold me (or uphold me) is to have my heart. You can't uphold me if you can't understand the intricacies of my heart. Think about it.

For Better or For Worse

"Thirty-three years and counting"

My husband and I met when we were just seventeen years old. We married each other when we were twenty-five. We have been married for over thirty years. Our marriage has certainly been the poster picture for the line, *"For better or for worse."*

When we met, I was a student at Florida A&M University. I still remember the announcement that came over the intercom that a gospel group was about to sing in the lobby. I absolutely loved gospel music and can sing a note or two. Lol. I made it my business to get there in time to hear the group sing. There he was; my knight in shining armor. But wait a minute God! This is not the order I put in! He was not tall *at all*. He wasn't light-skinned and his hair definitely wasn't long. What could this mean, could God know what we need better than we know ourselves? Well, I reckon so.

This short, brown-skinned low-hair-cut man could sing his rear off! The music had a magical power over me. His voice made him sound ten-feet-tall. His tone enlightened my life. I would see the sway of the hair of Samson as he would sway back and forth with the beat. Wow. I was smitten. And then his sense of humor was the icing on the cake. God knows laughter is vital to me. I really am silly myself. But then he had the greatest attribute that height, nor skin nor hair could supersede; and that was that he loved God with *all* his heart.

It was not long before I ran into him again on the sidewalk. At that time, I expressed to him how I wanted to be a part of their singing group. In the weeks to come he would pick me up for rehearsals driving that bronze Galaxy 500. Lol. *Ooo child!* I remember saying to him one day, "Does your speedometer only have one speed?" This man drove *ninety miles per hour!* I mean, he drove like a bat out of Hades! But even that didn't matter because; where ever he was flying off to I wanted to be right there with him.

Our relationship became the epitome of opposites attract. I was tall, he was short. I was quiet, and he was outspoken. And I mean *VERY* outspoken. There were days when I found it intolerable, but then there were other days when I knew in my heart he only spoke the things that I just had in my head but didn't have the courage to say. I secretly wished that I had at least a little bit of that gift. We shared many good times over the years, but it would not take long before we would be taken through the twist and turns in the Relationship Maze. During these times, we each saw what would be the worst of times. Boy did that relation*SHIP* turn. It tossed and turned, and almost sank like the Titanic. It is by the Grace of God that we have survived. We are both witnesses that there is no situation in any relationship that God can't help you to overcome.

The Marriage Relationship is hard work,
and you better come to work with your tools.
Your tools are forgiveness, compromise, the
fruit of the spirit, and especially love. These
tools can fix anything in a relationship.

For Richer or for Poorer

"The furniture move"

After moving to Atlanta to pursue life,
we moved in with his sister. We had a small
wedding at the Hyatt Hotel. I sometimes do
wonder to myself, "How could a church girl not
have a Church wedding?" But nevertheless,
that's neither here nor there.

At the beginning of our marriage we
didn't have much. We were just glad to have

each other. He worked for a hotel and I was a

nursing assistant. Eventually, our combined

salaries just did afford us the bare necessities of

food, clothing, and shelter. That shelter ended

up being a little two-bedroom house in walking

distance from his sister. We had a roof over our

head, but did not have a tap of furniture. We

found out one weekend that some of our college

friends were coming to Atlanta for a visit. We

certainly could not let them see us in this less

than wealthy state so we took a drastic measure.

Late that night we borrowed a sofa from his

sister. *HA!* I'm tickled right now just thinking

about it. Your neighbors are supposed to

borrow a cup a sugar or maybe even a light

bulb, but a SOFA? Lol! Yep, that's what we

did. We carried a huge sofa right down the street from her house to ours in the middle of the night. What a site! *Lordy, Lordy* the things we did to survive. We may not have had a lot of stuff, but we were happy.

The struggle would not always be like that. My husband's bold presence and outspokenness landed him a management position with the hotel. After I survived the drama of getting my nursing license, I never had a nursing job without a management title. Better jobs meant better incomes. We were soon enjoying the finer things in life. We still may not have been rich according to some standards, but I can say that we didn't want for much.

Til Death Do Us Part

"Two for the price of one"

As morbid as it may sound *til death do us part* is the deal you make when you get married. At this point in our marriage I was assured that we will surpass this juncture in the Relationship Maze. I don't think death is quite a subject you want to joke about; however, the devil must have thought one day there was a two for one sale on lives.

I am still in a little bit of disbelief over the fact that both my husband and I were sick unto death in the same year. Can you even begin to imagine what our daughters went

through watching both of their parents almost

die in the same year just months apart? That's

almost too much for any human being to bear,

let alone innocent children.

My husband ended up in ICU at the

brink of death with an intestinal disorder, and I

was practically given a death sentence with an

upper digestive disorder. The nature of the

illnesses is a moot point based on the magnitude

of the thought of death. I can't begin to tell you

the way the enemy wreaks havoc with one's

mind when you think that your spouse might not

be around. How will you survive without them?

Is your life insurance in order? Can you even

afford life insurance right now? What will it be like living alone? But then when you come back to your senses and remember the God that you serve, you grab life by the horns *and stop planning to die and start planning to live!*

Regardless of everything our marriage has endured there is one thing I know for sure. We will be together until *death do us part*. And this is how I know it. On one of the many occasions that I was hospitalized I can remember my husband standing at my bedside. I was hooked up to all kinds of tubes, and had just gotten upgraded from ICU to a regular hospital bed. My husband spoke God's word over me saying, "This sickness is not unto death." With those words, I knew two things. I knew that I will not die from this GI trouble, and I knew that whatever takes either of us out we will be together for the endurance.

Relationship Generality

Well we certainly can't talk about relationships without talking about learning and knowing how to simply relate to people in general. In the Relationship Maze of life, we are going to encounter all kinds of people. One of those groups I would like to stop and focus on for a moment. That group is called Difficult People. *Uggh!* What a group to have to contend with.

I have often thought about doing a book on the art of dealing with difficult people. One day I will. For whatever reason, God seems to have given me a knack for doing just that, dealing with difficult people. I mentioned in my chapter about emotions that I feared this very kind of person; however, I think there is a reason I have mastered getting along with them. You too will have to master that because some of the people we don't like here on earth will be spending eternity with us in Heaven. And I don't know about you, but I plan on going to Heaven and enjoying my stay.

Occasionally you may even find yourself in a romantic relationship with a difficult person. What an irony. How in the world does that happen? Who knows, but it does. Of course, we have all heard the theory that opposites attract. But have you also heard that like poles attract? So, which one is it? Could it be that there is a likeness in the opposition that we are drawn to? *Hmmm.* Perhaps the truth is that we don't necessarily attract or deflect either kind, but can more so be drawn to either. If we have attracted a difficult person in our lives then there are a few techniques we can use to manage a relationship with them.

Here's one technique. Put yourself in their shoes for a moment. When a difficult person is ranting, raving, or sulking you should listen to what they are *not* saying. I once heard a Pastor say, "The thing is never *the thing*," and believe you me it's not. That difficult person is saying things audibly. They may even send certain messages physically via body language. But all of that can sometimes be tricky. Learn how to listen deeper. Learn how to look deeper. What they're saying and how they're acting are mere clues as to what's really going on inside.

Probably one of the least effective ways to manage a relationship with a difficult person is to simply stuff and deny your own feelings. Time and time again it's been proven that this method of denial is just a temporary fix. It covers the wound temporarily, but the deep-

seated pain is always there. This often turns
into resentment. You may not even realize the
pain is there yourself until someone or
something comes along to expose it. When that
exposure happens its sort of like exhuming a
body that has been buried. The process of
decompensation has begun. As a good Coroner
can still perform an autopsy and divulge the true
cause of death, so can God exhume the
emotional hurts and pains you've buried deep
down inside and reveal the true sources of them.
All you must do is let Him perform the autopsy.

I recently had such an encounter while
sitting in a movie theater. Never once did I
meet the writer of the film, yet he wrote as if I

sat in the theater alone and he knew my story. At one point the words that flowed from the mouth of the woman on the screen seem to formulate some kind of emotional shovel. The shovel then traveled from the movie screen and rammed straight through me. It pierced deep down below the surface of my superficial cordial soul turning over and revealing thoughts and feelings I thought I had carefully and neatly buried. How could she know these things I felt? She was a fictitious character made up in the mind of a screenwriter. It was uncanny how well she knew me, how she knew my pain, how she spoke for me, how she cried for me. But this was only a movie, right? Somehow this encounter was a tremendous help for me. It aided me in finding my way through the Relationship Maze. I certainly do know that even just that acknowledgement of these feelings helps me to move past them and not allow them to interfere with my relationships with others. Sometimes all you must do is face it. Getting clear about your own pains and struggles can assist you with having better relationships with others.

Walking on Egg Shells

One day while cleaning my house I saw that my puppy had found an eggshell lying just near the trash. The eggshell had been broken by him into many other smaller pieces. As I cleaned up the pieces I was reminded of what it's like to have to communicate with someone who makes you feel you must walk as if you're walking on eggshells with them. You never know which word from your mouth will cause a crack. The revelation that God revealed to me regarding the egg could free you and I both of what I call the WOG Syndrome or the Walking on Eggshells Syndrome.

Let's think about the egg for a moment. The egg itself may have an outer shell that is hard, but the internal content of an egg is simply made of a liquid. The liquid itself is good, but you would not know it unless you were able to get to it. Here's a thought for you. We really

don't have to be afraid if the shell breaks,
because what's inside is greatness for sure.

Now you may ask what happens if you
crack the shell of an egg, and find that it has
been hard-boiled? In that case, just know that
for an eggs inner content to become hardened it
would have to have had an encounter with some
kind of heat over a period of time. This is ok
too.

With that thought I think we must
consider that people who have that hard-inner
content must have had some very heated
situations in their lives. Difficult situations can
certainly change the content of your inner most
being. This acknowledgement causes me to be

a little more compassionate for the *hard-boiled* person. Even if someone is hard-boiled, even a hard-boiled egg can be quite good. All you must do is put a little salt on it. Sometimes, all people need is to get their salt back. This requires that you give them some of yours. After all, we are supposed to be the "salt of the earth," right?

The ultimate revelation is that regardless of what we find on the inside of that cracked shell, it's all still good. The relationships we have with people are often a reflection of the relationship we have with God. When you are committed to God then that same relationship tends to transfer over into our relationship with people. When we have a strong love for God, we love people. When we are loyal to God, then for the most part we are loyal to people.

Having good relationships are vital to our lives. When God created the earth, there was only one thing that he said was *not* good. His words were "*It is not good that man should be alone.* (Gen. 2:18)." Not only should we be *in* relationships, but we should be in *good* relationships. So, what constitutes a good relationship? A good barometer can be based on the premise we've all heard, *"Association brings on assimilation."* Choose your friends and acquaintances carefully. Watch them from a distance first. Draw close to those who can take you to a higher plane, verses those who will take you under. Listen to your gut. Watch their character. We become much like the people we attach ourselves to and vice versa. Stop and take a moment to look at those closest to you. Do you see yourself? Do you even like what you see? Is it time to develop new relationships? If so, how do you do that?

To develop some new relationships there are some things you can do. Joining community groups or attending networking events is a good start. The internet offers all types of fun and safe meet-up type of groups. It gives one the opportunity to choose groups who have the same interest and passions as you do. Attend places and events where you would not normally go. This could expose you to a whole new group of associates who are on a whole different level. Set a goal to make three or four new friends each year. It's called networking and connecting.

On the opposite spectrum of relationships, it may be time for you to disconnect yourself from some people. Perhaps they have already served their purpose. Perhaps they are not willing to grow. They may bring a negative energy into your life that is not beneficial to your growth. There could be many reasons to cut the cord, and if you listen to your heart you will know who stays and who should go.

Finally let's discuss when it's time to keep someone close that other people don't like. The best words for this scenario is *all may not be lost*. I can certainly attest to this. I had someone close to me who was very beneficial to many things I do. I cannot argue that the person surely fell short on my behalf on many occasions. I decided not to throw this person totally and completely away. For whatever reason that worked for me. It is a grave injustice to try to force someone to dislike another person just because you don't like them. One man's junk is another man's gold and silver. There are certainly incidences where a person who is unproductive in one place can become the epitome of productivity in another place.

I have seen a Pastor go into a church that is not thriving and turn that same group of people around simply because he knows how to relate to them. That same person you may call your God-forsaken husband could be another woman's King. Somebody could take that same wife you call unworthy and pull the Queen out of her. Occasionally when we look at people we see them from where we are. This is simply to say think carefully before you decide to throw out that baby. It could be more valuable than you think.

In the world that we live in today a real friend is a valuable commodity. According to our social media status we may have hundreds or even thousands of friends electronically, yet in real life we may only have just one or two. A real friend is that person who won't judge us when we do stupid stuff. We can talk to them and tell them all our secrets. They listen to us and we know we have been heard. They always seem to have just the right words to comfort us when we are down and celebrate our wins with us when we are victorious. Real friends are friends for life. We don't have to speak to them every day to be reminded of our friendship. Although we have heard that *blood is thicker than water*, occasionally a friendship can be a more committed relationship than even our own kin.

Weathering the Storm

Every relationship on earth has its challenges. This is regarding whatever the nature of your relationship is. It could be between husbands and wives, parents and children, sisters and brothers, workers and coworkers and even pastors and congregants. No relationship is immune to the potential for conflict. This is because we are all human and have been purposely made different by God.

We are each wonderfully and fearfully made. Each of us is unique in our own right. We are like puzzle pieces on the earth, and from time to time the pieces that come together simply do not fit. It is difficult to watch when the pieces don't fit and there is major conflict. When some parties don't understand how to deal with conflict in a relationship it can often result in adverse scenarios such as abuse.

I do want to say here that even church folks can fall into this conflict trap. I have unfortunately witnessed both physical and verbal abuse among the saints within the Church. This certainly is not new according to the scriptures. The Apostle Paul had to call out two women in the Church who could not get along. He could bring to their attention how their conflicts were impacting the ministry.

Here's a worthy note. What you do at home will certainly be revealed by the spirit at Church. May I use an analogy? Have you ever driven by a building and felt the spirit of the building? You can actually tell if the activity is alive and vibrant in the building verses a building that seems dark and desolate even when it is occupied. The same way we can sense that presence in a building is the same way people can sense the presence or absence of peace in your relationships. It will not matter how loving and kind you speak to each other in public. Your spirit will always speak louder than your words.

If you are having trouble coping with your feelings I recommend reading the chapter on emotions to gain a better understanding of self. We must learn to understand the mathematics of relationships in order to make it through the Relationship Maze.

My husband and I can teach somebody else how to weather a marital storm for sure. And I've lived long enough to have weathered my fair share of general relationships too. If I had to give three good pieces of advice on how to weather relationship storms these are the things I would say.

1. **Stay Close:** In a natural storm, the safest and calmest place is in the eye of the storm. Stay close to each other and do not focus on extraneous things. It will only create more arguments when you focus outside of the present concern and bring up old matters.

2. **Stay Covered:** No normal person goes out into a storm without proper covering. Use prayer to cover yourself, your spouse, or that other person in the relationship. This covering will protect each of you, and hide you so the enemy can't see ammunition that he may use to create more conflict. The couple, the

friendship, and even the family that
prays together stays together.

3. **Stay Inside:** The safest place in a storm
   is inside until the storm passes. Don't
   ever seek relief for the turmoil going on
   in your relationship by going outside to
   yet another relationship to seek advice.
   This will only compound the issues at
   hand. Talk to each other, seek council,
   and seek God for answers. Remember
   he is the one who spoke to the storm and
   said the words, "Peace be still," and the
   storm calmed.

The Relationship Maze is surely one filled
with ongoing surprises because we as

individuals are constantly changing every day.
The more we evolve, the more the Relationship
Maze gets interesting. We must become
flexible enough to flow with the evolution.

4

The Spiritual Maze

When God Speaks

So how do you know you are in a
Spiritual Maze? The answer to that would be,
"When you find yourself in a place where you
are wondering what is God's desire and
direction for your life." It would be so easy if
we could just call God up and ask him, and then
get an audible answer. Right? Unfortunately,
it's not that easy. The difficulty comes in trying

to decipher the voice of God amongst the so many other voices that are in the atmosphere.

It's not often that I would tell someone that I've heard the voice of God; however, on *this* particular day I definitely heard the instruction of God to, "Go to Lenox Mall." Now, of course you would have to be from around here (Atlanta) to understand that Lenox is the area of town where the more affluent live. Hearing these instructions, I shrugged it off knowing that Lenox had nothing I could afford at the time. The more I resisted the urge, the stronger the urge came to go to Lenox. I finally gave in and headed for the mall. Strolling through the mall, I wandered into one particular store and saw that the clothing items all started at $800 per item. This only confirmed for me that I was certainly in the wrong place for my budget.

As I attempted to leave the mall I spotted an elderly woman. She was barefoot and dressed in her pajamas as she walked pass the mall. How could hundreds of cars pass by her and no one stop to give her aid? It was certainly an extremely odd image, especially in this part of town. With my long history of working with the elderly as a nurse, I immediately knew that this woman suffered from Alzheimer's. I pulled my car over to her. I backed down the street where she walked and I spoke to the lady. I asked here where she was going, and she muttered a few nonsensical words mixed with a little, "I'm just headed up there." Now I knew for sure she was lost. I also knew someone must have been looking for her. So, I helped the woman to my car, and then tried to find a house that would let me use their phone. Yet another strange thing was about to happen. As I drove I looked at an array of nearby homes, and I randomly picked one. A woman came to the door and saw the elderly woman. The woman immediately called the ailing woman by name. Her son then walked up behind her in the home and calls *my* name. What an improbable occurrence! It turned out that the home owners' son actually worked with me on a previous nursing assignment. The owner also knew the husband of the elderly woman I had just found. She even had the man's contact information. The husband of the ailing woman was immediately notified, and we all waited patiently for him to arrive.

Of course, he had great relief now that his wife—who wandered off—had been safely found. After some conversation, the husband hired me as their private duty nurse, and I cared for both for two (2) years. Just suppose I had continued to resist that urge. Perhaps God really does speak to people.

Is God speaking to you? What have you clearly heard in your spirit repeatedly? You know you've heard God, but now you're afraid to act on it. You're at a place where you don't want to tell anybody about what God has said. You're dealing with the fear that it may not come to pass, or others may not agree with what you say you've heard. Who am I talking too?

Let's hit it right on the nail here. How can you really know that it was God who spoke to you, and not just your own subconscious mind or wishful thinking? *Man!* What a great Segway to the thought I'd like to share now. It's about wishful thinking, and I promise it will bring you right back to the voice of God.

"I Wish I Had…"

Everybody knows that I love children, and one day I was babysitting my five-year-old niece. There's one thing you can count on kids to do, and that's to say interesting things. They have not yet developed their inner filters so what comes up comes out. I know a few adults who are still working on that. Lol. Knowing that kids are miniature human recorders they have the potential to rewind and do playback of everything they have seen you do or heard you say. Wow! And who can get mad at these cute little faces and those cute little voices of truth? All you can do is just pick your face up off the floor and keep right on moving. Since I work with kids a lot, you better know that I have had them say a few things to me.

Nevertheless, everything a kid says is not always embarrassing. Occasionally the words from a child's mouth can be quite enlightening and empowering. We have all heard the phrase, "Out of the mouth of babes," which really refers to those empowering kinds of words.

On one day, I was taking my niece home. She rode in the back seat in her little safety seat as required. During the ride, she asked me a question, *"Auntie can I use your phone to play the game on it."* Of course, I didn't have a problem with that. Thank God for these mechanical babysitters who keep kids preoccupied when we need them to stay quiet. Lol. I told her, "Sure that would be fine." As I passed my phone back to her she asked yet another question, "Auntie, do you think you could buy me a cell phone for Christmas next year? That way I won't have to keep borrowing other people's phones to play with, and I will have my own."

Now before I get into the real revelation of our conversation let me help you understand the mind of a child. Most children have no clue that parents must pay bills, let alone on the phones they request. In their immature minds people just give you whatever you ask for. At this point my niece has already exemplified and spoken of an empowering revelation. God bless the child that's got his own! Right? Later was the revelation that *really* spoke to me. My niece was quietly playing a game on my phone, but as she played she began to verbalize a statement repeatedly. She said, *"I wish I had a phone. I wish I had a phone. I wish I had a phone."* Every time she said it, her words were doing something to me. I started thinking in my head about what I could do to help her get a phone. She's a great kid and the more she spoke her request the more I wanted to grant her what she asked for. Then my eyes welled up with tears as I heard God say, "That's how much I love you.

That's how much I want to give you what you desire."

Listen, whatever it is that you want from God I pray that you keep it before Him in prayer. Keep making your request known in faith. God loves us as a parent loves their child. No parent would withhold a child's desire from them, especially if the child continues to do the right thing in life and continuously petition in faith.

I shared that story with my own daughters and our church family. I learned a great lesson from listening to this child that day. What she taught me was to go back and begin to ask God for those things I had started asking for long ago, but gave up on because I gave out of faith. My daughter and I started making a joke of it. One day while walking through the mall I saw these really cute boots and I began saying, "I wish I had those boots. I wish I had those boots," and one day my daughter surprised me with those boots. It was because she heard me say it several times. I thought to myself in that moment, "Wow, it actually works!"

Now there's another revelation to this too. God is not a genie; however, what He has the power to do is to place multiple people in your life to help you obtain the hopes and dreams in your vision. There came a point where not only was I trying to get my niece a phone, but my daughter and my niece's father was searching high and low for a phone. By this time, everyone had heard this little girl's request, because she kept repeating it in faith.

Here's the revelation: God can position a multitude of people and resources to come to your beckon call. It'll come from the north, south, east, and west if you just keep on requesting in faith. You just must put it out there in the atmosphere. Cast and project your vision. *GOD DOES ANSWER.* What do *you* want from God? What dreams and visions has He placed on the inside of you to desire? You may not hear His audible voice, but you will see the manifestation of his responses in many ways if you just keep on asking. One of the greatest lessons you can learn while down here in this Spiritual Maze is this: know how to ask in faith. Realize that nothing materializes in the natural unless you ask in the spirit and by faith first.

So why does God answer and speak to His children? If you are a parent then you already know the answer to this. Why do you think so many parents break their necks and their bank accounts in order to get that GI Joe with the Kungfu Grip or that Cabbage Patch Doll that went viral long before the term Viral meant more than a disease?

Do you know the feeling that a parent gets when they've given their child the desire of

their heart? Can you imagine how your
Heavenly Father will feel on the day you receive
that thing you've been praying for? I've had the
opportunity to be in those shoes so I do have
some idea of what God might feel like as our
father. I have a daughter who plays the
keyboard, but as a working parent even with a
great job I could not afford that $2500 keyboard
she wanted. I didn't have the money, but God
surely did bless me with another gift. That gift
was the gift of writing so I wrote a grant for it.

While I was at work one day I just so
happen to look up and see that one of the
Atlanta Falcons were starting a foundation for
kids in the Arts called "Pick Your Passion." I

listened intently for the contact information and wrote them a letter. In the letter, I told them all about my little musical genius who needed a real keyboard.

They later told me that when he got the letter he and a friend were riding around together, and when they read my letter they said, "This is exactly what we are looking for!" A short time later we all went to the Gala where my daughter would be presented with the keyboard. We had to trick her though and tell her that I was getting yet another community service award. Lol. When the football player approached the microphone, he began telling a story about a person. My daughter was standing next to me, and I was watching her face change as she began to realize that the story they were telling was about her. They began talking about this girl who loved music and used to put on her daddy's boots and walk around the house carrying a curtain rod as her baton. To say the least, that became a reality for the next two years. As he ended his speech, a man began walking up behind her carrying a $2500 Motif 8 that was all hers! *GOD DOES ANSWER PRAYER!* "Ask and it shall be given to you *(Luke 11:9)."*

Your Heavenly Father needs to hear from you repeatedly. It's not that He can't hear but it's more so, "How bad do you want it?" By the way, this same child of mine is now traveling and touring the world as the keyboardist for two (2) Grammy award winning R&B artists. The lesson is this: in the Spiritual Maze, you'll quickly realize that your mobility, advancement, and promotion are contingent upon your asking according to the will of God. If you ask long enough you will receive. This is what the fundamentals of church should teach us. It should teach us how to lean and depend on God and His word for the answers. Unfortunately, many people have missed this factor about church.

It is unfortunate that many people attend church in a mode to *inspection* instead of *expectation.* It is so easy to get caught up in what we see in the natural. I know how frustrating it has been sometimes in the past when I've preached my guts out, and then someone says, "That was a beautiful outfit you had on." C'mon, I mean *REALLY?* Could it be that we say we are seeking God and His will for our lives, yet we keep missing the obvious? Isaiah 55:6 says, "Seek the Lord while *He* may be found, call on Him while *he* is near." God is much closer than you think, and you are closer to your destination than you think. You are too close to give up now. You've just got to stay focused on the main thing while on this spiritual journey.

I can imagine you may be feeling that you're lost or stuck during your Spiritual Maze. I know what it's like to feel you have been in the same place for a long time. I know what it's like to feel you have no direction, and the only thing worse than no direction is too many directions. I've been there too. It tempts you to quit. It woos you into the immobile stage. But that is the very nature of a maze. Sometimes, there are so many choices and routes to go, each of them are filled with the uncertainty of where you might end up. Others have just a few options regarding direction, yet you're still stuck with the nagging, "I don't know what will happen," if you choose either way. Perhaps you are that person who has been given multiple gifts, and you are not sure which one of those

gifts will lead you out of your Spiritual Maze to

victory. One thing for sure, it is difficult to try

to go in several directions at one time. You'll

split yourself in halves or more if you attempt to

do that. You'll have to learn to discern the

voice of God. Follow the voice of God. In

other words, follow the unction of your spirit

man. That's the leading of the Holy Spirit

showing you where to go. It's the healthy and

uplifting thing that you can't help but do.

That's where God is calling you to. And if it

just so happens to be multiple things, know that

God will give you the grace to focus on them

all. You'll know you don't have the grace to do

it all when frustration and unproductivity sets in.

And get this; sometimes the grace comes through the mechanism of organization.

I say these things as one with many gifts. This is certainly not to inflate my own ego, but to demonstrate my understanding of others in the same dilemma. As a nurse, a pastor, singer, writer, producer, & director, I still have more days than I care to count where I feel, "there's something more. I still haven't walked into the main thing, the main destination or purpose."

It's probably ironic that I listed all my gifts, but never once did I mention that I'm a dancer. Now this is really an interesting story. How in the world does a person with no professional dance training create one of the city's most awarded dance programs and even

perform Off Broadway? Sometimes, you've got

to go with the unction. You've got to flow with

the current of God's spirit. Many times, God is

leading you to the very place of your destiny if

you'd pay attention. And many times, you don't

even have to be qualified for it. You don't have

to be formerly trained as a dancer to be a great

dancer. Some people just have a natural born

God-given gift. But that wasn't even me. I

wasn't even a good dancer. But here's why I

feel God gave me this assignment.

I always loved working with children so

I quit my job *(once again)* to pursue my desire

to work with children. I started a home child

care business. To keep the learning environment interesting I went out and bought a ballet tutu, and I told the kids we are going to dance! When I presented it to the children suddenly, I now had some kind of magical power.

I recall the children saying to me, "*Mrs. Pat, if we eat our vegetables can we put on our tutu?*" Wow! Who knew this kind of power was possible? In the days to come I would find myself driving down one of the main streets in Atlanta. It was during the Easter Season when many churches would drape a cross outside with a purple fabric to represent the crucified Christ. *Whew!* I still get a little bit overwhelmed when

I think about what happened to me on that day. As I passed this church, I noticed the fabric that draped the cross out front. Then something just came over me. I was overwhelmed with a tremendous feeling of despair when I thought of the pain my Lord suffered. I can hardly think about it even now without the thoughts taking me back to that moment. Clearly, I heard God speak to my spirit that day and the instruction was, *"Now go back and have the children Dance the story of my Son."*

Immediately with—no dance training, no costumes, and no money—just an unction from God the production *Resurrection* was born. The production transformed from a

Saturday afternoon church play to a major theater production seen on several professional stages in the city of Atlanta; including the Rialto Theatre itself. I have since been blessed to celebrate twenty years of doing professional children's musical theater productions and I have founded the nonprofit school of performing arts called *KIDDS Dance Project Inc* that houses the dancers who perform in these musicals.

So, why me Lord? My friends who went to nursing school with me also asked that question of me. How is it that you went from nursing to dancing? I do have the answer and I want you to listen very carefully, because the answer may help give you some direction through your maze right now.

As the production of *Resurrection* grew I could cross paths with many whom I felt to be far more qualified to manage a dance program than myself. I tried to give the program away to someone who was a professional dancer, but God simply would not allow it. I was about to put God in the same frame of mind he was in when Moses kept telling him to send his brother Aaron instead. Aaron was a much better spokesperson than Moses. There's no doubt about that. He had the gift, but he did not have the calling. Even when he would go out with his brother Moses he could only speak words that Moses told him to according to the word of the Lord.

Every man, woman and child on earth has a calling and a purpose from God on their life. And each person will—at some point or another—feel inadequate as it relates to fulfilling their purpose. I know exactly what that feels like. Having been chosen by God to bring forth a major dance musical I questioned why God would not give the assignment to the person with professional dance training. It was made very clear to me later when the production had become a paramount success. I could only give God the glory taking no credit for myself.

Knowing that I had no formal training, it had to be all God.

Yet another occasion came when God called on me once again to bring the community a group to educate people about the Arts. As I moved forward with God's direction I encountered one in the group whom I felt should have been called because of their professional background. At this point God must have been becoming as angered with me as he had with Moses. Remember Moses wanted God to choose Aaron instead for the task God wanted him to do. One day I preached a message called *That Call Was for Me*. After a while God would make it very clear to me again why this dance

calling was for me. The person who had the
professional training in our Arts group decided
they had to be guaranteed a certain number of
people in the audience to proceed with the
vision. This was the moment I knew that the
call was for me and not them. God knew that in
my heart I would teach the people whether there
was one or one hundred in the audiences of our
shows. Numbers didn't matter to me more than
the mission and the vision.

I understand now how God can use one
person to change the lives of an entire nation. It
has been said that one person can change your
life for the rest of your life. I would propose
that subsequently you could be that one person

to change another person's life. At this juncture let me encourage that Pastor who may be discouraged by repeatedly seeing a small group. Know that you are planting a seed that someone else may water. You are doing a work that cannot be rewarded only in numbers or financial blessing alone. Although these are great manifestations and markers of success, they are not the only ones. It's also about how many hearts you've sparked on fire for Christ, and how many lives were changed for the better. If you're achieving this, your work is not in vain.

Let's check out Exodus 4. Moses is very clear regarding the request God has made of him. He understands that God wants him to go to Pharaoh and tell Pharaoh to, "Let my people go." In hearing the call Moses begins to give God excuses as to why he cannot adequately perform the task. He tells God that he is not an eloquent speaker. Moses also feels his brother Aaron would be a far better choice because Aaron is such a smooth talker. He's more articulate.

But be careful what you propose to God and what you ask him for. God soon gives Moses his request and allows Aaron to go forth with him. During them going; however, Aaron could only speak to Moses what God says and Moses must speak in verbatim to Pharaoh. God has put the gift inside of you and not in that person you are trying to send in your place.

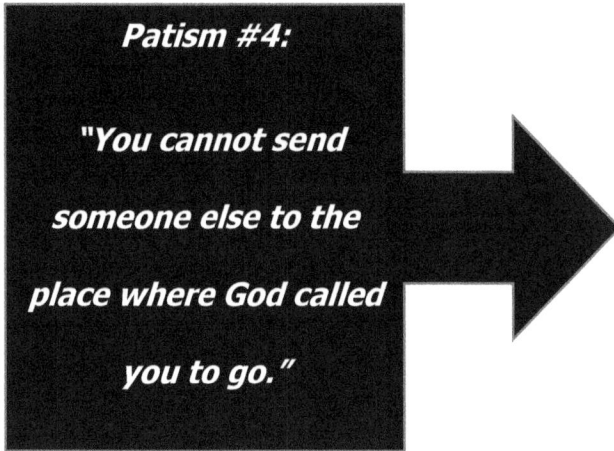

> **Patism #4:**
>
> **"You cannot send someone else to the place where God called you to go."**

God has already equipped you, delivered you, supplied you and anointed you and you only for the task. for the task. Nobody else can do it like God would have you to do it. There is something already in your DNA that makes you the one. Something in your character that makes you the one. Something in your walk with God that makes you the one. THE CALL WAS FOR YOU!

Moses eventually finds out that Aaron is more trouble than he is worth. Thank God for occasionally not giving us what we ask for because he knows what is best for us. That's what a loving parent does. Let's be clear, God wasn't dealing with Moses' excuses as to why he wasn't good enough. Look deeper. He was dealing with Moses' insecurities. But God knew what it would take to build Moses' confidence. He also knows what it will take for you. Moses' biggest fear was that Pharaoh would see him as weak and powerless. He thought this would not get him the victory God wanted. God rectifies this insecurity by showing Moses three demonstrations of his divine power. He shows Moses his staff being turned into a serpent, his hand becoming diseased with leprosy then restored, and the water being turned to wine. With these demonstrations, the confidence of Moses is increased and he becomes ready to go forth in his calling.

There are four principles in this lesson to help your confidence boost as it relates to answering your call:

Principle #1: Look back at the miracles God already performed in your life.

There are no obstacles the enemy can create that God's power cannot overcome. Nothing can hinder you from going forth in your call: not finances, nor health, nor family, nor naysayers of any sort. God still has the same power he used to bring you through before to bring you through today.

Principle #2: Be willing to be used by God.

It is an honor and a Blessing to be chosen by God for a task. Answer his call and go forth with the confidence of God. Trust His decision to call you for the task.

Principle #3: Know that God can use anybody.

In verse 11, when Moses tells God his mouth and tongue are slow and not good enough, God reminds him that He made his mouth and He is a God that can use you beyond your shortcomings.

Principle #4: Make sure God is with you.

In verse 12, God told Moses, "I will be *with* thy mouth." That which seemed powerless now becomes powerful when God is *with* it. Moses realized Gods presence gave his mouth power. We can all benefit from that same knowledge. You want to make sure God is *with* your money, your marriage, your job, your health and any part of your being that God desires to use. "For *with* God nothing shall be impossible." The power of God is with you! Go forth because "THAT CALL WAS FOR YOU!"

Now if that didn't open a door for you I don't know what will. It certainly made things clear to me. I did ask God, "Why me?" He helped me to understand that if a professional dancer put the dance together there might be the risk of someone saying, "Look what I've done." But since I knew I had no dance skills, I was and still am forced to say, "Look what *God* has done!" God will always make sure He gets the glory.

The Wilderness Maze

Again, I want to encourage those of you who have multiple gifts. I once heard a teaching on the Garden of Eden and how the Garden had four streams that fed into it. This says to me that it's ok to have multiple streams of income and even multiple gifts. In fact, multiple streams of income may even be a necessity during these times. You just never know when one of the streams might dry up. Let's think about this, if there is monetary value in each of your gifts then can you imagine the kind of wealth you'd walk in every day? When we think of it like that then it makes me feel almost ashamed to ever have used the word *broke*.

That term probably better describes our spirits at any given time as *broken.*

It takes so much intestinal fortitude to keep pushing and stay inspired when things look bleak. What happens when it seems like the walls of the maze are caving in on you? We all have experienced a time like that in our lives. Isn't it ironic how soon we forget how God brought us through every trial before? Isn't it amazing how quickly we forget how God has equipped us for the journey? Funny how new trials create a state of amnesia. We get so caught up in the present pains that we totally forget the past times we've made it through.

This must be how the children of Israel felt during their time of wandering in the Wilderness Maze. My wilderness was once during an eleven month stretch of being unemployed. Periodic unemployment is just one of the natures of the beast in my line of work. I never know when God is going to take my patients on home to Glory.

I had been working as a private duty nurse for a police officer who was hit by a drunk driver. I will never know what kind of personality he had prior to his injury; however, his present state left much to be desired. The accident left him unable to speak so he had to communicate with me via a special computer.

Thou he could not vocalize the word himself, I could clearly understand the computer each time I was called a nigger.

Be very careful of the kind of prayers you pray in the wilderness. I prayed for it to all be over. I grew to hate that job. Now I know that *hate* is a very strong word, but I did. If I can just be honest for a moment. I was miserable working on that job, and no amount of money relieved the tremendous despair I felt as I drove to it every day for five years. Not only was it emotionally humiliating, it was the most back breaking work I've ever done in my life. I will always remember the night I got that phone call saying, "He's gone." The misery of the work was finally over, but the misery of a prolonged period of unemployment had just begun.

Man! Many of us have been there. The badgering and harassment of bill collectors calling is overwhelming. The psychological and emotional distress is unyielding. It's a part of the entire maze of life that no one ever wants to have to walk through. Being in the depths of this maze impacts every iota of your being, mentally, physically, emotionally and spiritually.

We can all recall the Children of Israel having their moment when they verbalized their discontent with the wilderness experience. If you keep someone in pain long enough they will eventually cry out.

May I just speak out loud for a few of us? How many times did we think, "Where is God?" I attended church every Sunday without question. Even if I didn't have transportation I used the same ingenuity to get myself to church that I used to get to work on Mondays. I'm a genuine worshipper. I don't need a praise and worship leader to provoke me to give God praise. I'm the first one standing during worship while others sit like a knot on a log not moved by anything God has done for them. I often think how selfish! Can you not just give God these few moments of praise? During this hard season, I still paid my tithe even when I couldn't pay my bills. But still I was asking, "Where is God?" At some point, the God in me rose above all questions. The word soon came alive in me and I was reminded that all things worked together for the good. I remembered that the things that might seem like incantation are just a part of the preparation for what God has for me.

Looking back, I would not have changed a single thing. Even the pages of this book would not exist without the mazes I've encountered in life, especially the Spiritual and Wilderness Maze. Do you get it now? The Spiritual Maze *is* the Wilderness Maze. You learn to find God in the burning bush, on the top of the mountain, down in the valley, and even in the prisons of complacency, inadequacy, and the like as you walk through the wilderness. These encounters in the wilderness will bring you closer to God and increase your spiritual walk with God. Someone going through their maze will read these words and their hope will be restored. They'll move on knowing that God will also bring them out of their maze. When God brought the Children of Israel out of Egypt he did not get out of the release business. HE's still releasing and relieving people today. God surely has the power to restore and bring anybody out of any situation. I hear God saying right now, "Tell the people to look around and start packing the things they want to take with them because they are about to be released from their wilderness experience. AMEN!"

Know Thyself

During the early days of my ministry, my husband and I knew we were called to pulpit ministry. We started the church in our home as just a bible study. It would not take long before we would move out and start the actual church in a building location. In the beginning, many would come and we'd welcomed them all regardless of their intentions. Even saying that I don't believe in my heart that any person purposely came to the church with ill-gotten intentions; however, it became evident that there were those who came with their own agenda. Those personal agendas would soon create havoc in the church. At one point, there seemed to be two churches with two heads on the same body. The other church or group of people decided there would be a Women's Conference. I attended for peace sake. My attendance was against my better judgement. I was so spiritually weak and immature that I could not stand up for what was right. God forgive me. I remember leaving the hotel on the last day of the conference and being overwhelmed with this tremendous feeling of depression. As we used to say during my college days, "My spirit was vexed."

Now I can't say that someone else won't ever try to come in and press their agenda. One thing I know for sure is that nobody will ever again take that kind of advantage over us because we now know who we are. Be sure to know thy self on this spiritual journey. When you know who you are it will help you to understand where you are in the maze of life. Any uncertainty about who you are in Christ will always open the door for the enemy to come in and try to shake your foundation. Be sure to know yourself and be certain. It's the enemy's job to trick us into thinking that the things God promised us are not true. If he can shake our worlds enough, then maybe he can shake God's word in us. Not so

Devil! It's too late now. God's word is rooted

and grounded within me and in you.

5

The Emotional Maze

I recently heard a pastor preaching a message, and in the message, he talked about the stomach having a brain of its own. Apparently, he had done his homework and I didn't take the time to do any additional research of my own; however, just listening to it brought new meaning to the words *gut feeling*. It was his premise that our feelings and emotions occur within our bellies. Just listening to those words took me back to the scriptures where it says, *"Out of your belly shall flow rivers of living waters (John 7:38)."* I do believe that our deep thoughts and feelings are rooted deep within our gut.

Most of us know if you had to choose between what you felt in your heart and what you felt in your gut; your gut (or house of intuition) probably would not lead you wrong. I would rather follow someone who had a *gut feeling* than one who had a heart feeling. You know, the heart is sick. "Who knows it," the Bible says. No one can figure out the heart. Feeling the truth of this also helps me to understand why it was so important for the enemy to attack my gut. One thing I know for sure is that I certainly do have *gut feelings.* In the spiritual realm those *gut feelings* are summed up as discernment, and that I have for sure.

The problem—however—is having a spirit of discernment but not being able to express that which you have discerned. Another problem is the fear to express what you have discerned. The fear comes with the fear of retaliation when one speaks the truth. I had a *gut feeling* that one day God would use everything that has happened in my life for his glory. Don't you know that everybody around me didn't agree with that? Nevertheless, it is with that thought that I can press through every pain and every moment of suffering. I know that I have experienced the full gamut of emotions. Everything from the sadness and despair that accompanies chronic illness to the irony of a moment of humor thinking about how funny it is that God would use the devastations to push me right into my destiny.

As a child, I can remember the old people singing a song, "We will understand it better by and by." Too many times we have felt emotional pain and never understood why. All we knew is that it hurt. *Bad.* And sometimes we could not tell people just how hurt we were. So instead of talking about it, we harbored it. Let me tell you what happens when you harbor feelings. You may not have spoken specifically about your pain, but you still spoke. Let me share something with you.

I have already mentioned that I am a nurse, but I did not mention that I spent about eighteen years working in the field of behavioral health. Not to mention that although I failed the Nursing State Board exams multiple times, I never failed the section of Psychiatry. I always passed that section with flying colors. The reason for that is because I seem to have always had a good grasp on the psychology of human behavior. My interpersonal relation skills are pretty good as well. I seem to be able to anticipate a person's behavioral response as well as decipher their feelings even when they can't. Sometimes you just need somebody to give you permission to feel what you are feeling.

If you could visualize your feelings and emotions, it would certainly create one of the most complex parts of the life maze. The walls would be taller than ever, making it most difficult to get over some things and they would seem to have no beginning and no ending.

Speaking of the walls, I once had a friend that I would jokingly climb over an imaginary wall every time I got ready to speak to her. It was somewhat comical to her because she knew I was simply demonstrating the fact that she had put up imaginary walls around herself to protect herself from the pains of this world. She was always so very depressed. She was never able to find her way through the sadness and one day it tragically ended her life.

We must understand that there is a marked difference between sadness and depression. Sadness is a temporary emotional downward pause whereas depression is an emotional downward spiral. It's the kind of funk that you cannot pull yourself out of without help or even divine intervention. As a pastor with a nursing license, I have occasionally seen many people who have needed more than just prayer but professional counseling too. I believe that it is our responsibility as pastors and church leaders. A major part of our responsibility is to be able to recognize the signs when someone has become emotionally unstable. Sometimes this mood behavior can be masked as hyper religious behavior. This is a behavior that may be inappropriately used as a coping mechanism. *Poor God.* Folk have blamed all kinds of stuff on Him that He had nothing to do with. Anytime you feel God has told you to cause harm to someone to relieve your feelings of pain, rejection, insecurity and the mix of emotional turmoil *that ain't God boo!* I must give credit to my dear friend Gina for always saying those words. Lol.

As a human being we must learn to listen to and master our emotions. Emotions are a strong entity, and if we are not careful an out of control emotional state will dictate your every move negatively. Every emotion has a conversation, behavior, and personality of its own. Haven't you ever heard someone say, "She was just not herself today." Let me explore just a few emotions that are common to man.

Anger

First let's look at the anger emotion. As you travel through the Emotional Maze you will recognize this wall by its many layers. Its surface layer speaks anger, but it hides and covers several other layers of emotions such as hurt, rejection, frustration and humiliation. Anger tends to rise to the surface as a shield to protect us from other feelings. It often temporarily aims at aiding a person in ignoring their true feelings for a while.

Fear

Fear is an emotion I could write a book on. I confess that I have always been a *scary cat.* That's probably another oxymoron. Genuinely cats are known for their "I don't care attitude." They rarely seem bothered and if they jump when you approach them it's not out of fear but more of a get away from me attitude. You can tell that they can also care less about your feelings or response to their negativity. And that's why I prefer puppies today. Lol

According to today's psychology, the emotion of fear is a sense of dread that alerts you of the possibility that your physical self might be harmed. This could also include the mental and emotional realms as well.

I have always been afraid of scary people, places and scary movies. I never watch a scary movie; at least not before bedtime. I have a fear of having scary dreams that may seem too real. My biggest fear—through all my life—has been with my communicating with scary people. Scary people—to me—are those who are mean and rude. You know them; they're the bullies and intimidators.

I have yet another confession. I have taken advantage of the presence of this book and written about things I would never have had the courage to speak about on a public platform. Those things are hidden on the pages of this book and perhaps only I know what specific things they are.

Writing is such a liberating gift. It's just you, God, and the pen. Together you can allow your true emotions to rest on the paper. Writing is a perfect way that you can get through the Emotional part of the Maze. Whatever emotion you are feeling can be laid to rest right there in those words on the paper. The pages have some sort of magical power. They hold on to what you feel, through the words you write. And when you come back to read them, those emotions come back to life. It could even be years later, and the same emotions that were captured when writing will be there on those pages waiting for you.

I'm tempted to take a little bit of a side street and talk about the fact that emotions not only speak, but they are also contagious. The phone rings and it's that negative person again. Thank God for caller ID. Right? As soon as you see the name you already know the content of the conversation. What tragedy is it going to be this week? Who hurt you now? You hear the words from an old TV show playing a sound tract in the background. Gloom, doom and tragedy on me. Deep dark depression, excessive misery, if it weren't for bad luck I'd have no luck at all. Blah. Blah. Blah. Same old story just a different day. Right? Yes, misery does love company. Miserable feelings and emotions love to commiserate with other miserable emotions. It's as if they try to meet up for lunch and feed off each other. This means you must be careful not to feed into your negative emotions. And don't feed into those that come from others as well.

The way to counter act these negative emotions of misery and desperation are with words of victory. When a person tries to take you around a negative emotional curve in the Emotional Maze, perhaps it's a good idea for you to take the lead. Turn the conversation around immediately by speaking words of gratitude and victory. There are far greater things happening in a person's life than disaster. You could start focusing on something like; just the mere fact that they had the breath to make the call says that whatever happened they survived it. Here's a key: if you speak well of your life then eventually the positive will overtake the negative. Your world forms around your emotional state. Your emotional

state gives birth to your reality and perspective.
Let's also make mention that the more you
speak positive to a negative person, the further
away you'll make them run or the more you'll
cause them to change. It won't take them long
to figure out you are not willing to feed their
misery. Misery is allergic to gratitude and
positivity. Misery is just a capsule that holds a
conglomerate of other feelings and emotions.
This can be so complex at times that we cannot
tell where one emotion ends and another begins.
We might find ourselves in a love-hate
relationship. With it being too complicated for
us to decipher, it's just sometimes easier to bury
these feelings. Once buried then these feelings
and emotions help us to turn some corners and

press our way a little bit further through the

Emotional Maze, even if it's not the truth.

Believe me, to not acknowledge these

feelings are equivalent to burying a body and

never placing a headstone on it. No headstone

might say to the natural eye that it never

happened, but the stench of a buried body of

emotions would still reveal itself in other ways.

On days when your attitude stinks it can

just be the aroma of those buried feelings. Your

divorce could just be the stench of those buried

feelings. Your dysfunctional relationship with

your child could simply just be the stench of

those feelings that you buried years ago. So, I

compel you to **give those buried feelings the**

finest headstones available. PAIN.

REJECTION. FEAR. INSECURITY. Call

them what they are. Acknowledge what it was.

Your ability to recognize it takes away its power

over you, and it puts the power over your

emotions back into your hands.

Patism #5:

"Never invite a cook to the dinner."

I believe it is important that we protect

our emotions, but we must occasionally put

them out there at our own risk. Especially

during these times of social media. These types of platforms are some of the riskiest places to share your feelings and emotions. Since we live in a world of brevity we don't always get to share the entire story. That means when we make those brief statements the readers get the option of assuming they know what brought you to that feeling. Sometimes their assumptions can be far from the truth. I have recently seen some high profiled people get *massacred* in the media because of their stated feelings and emotions. I have also seen some of these same people go back in retrospect and try to give people a little more information so that others might gain a different perspective on how the reader feels about them.

I recently felt the brunt of what happens in this case. Someone missed the point of what I was called to do for my life, and my feelings were CRUSHED. It really took me a moment to get over it and I honestly am still trying to work through that a little. I have even asked myself, why did that hurt so badly? I confess, *I CAN BE A WUSS AT TIMES!* Even as a child I would cry at the drop of a hat. I always felt I would never be a good salesperson. *I HATE SALES.* My fear is not the sale. It's the rejection when people say that word, *"NO.* I don't like or want what you have to offer." Now how unrealistic is it for me to think that everyone will like and want what I have? That ain't gonna be the case even if it's something they really need. That's just life.

Remember when you were told, "Don't cry over spilled milk?" Well I guess I didn't get that memo. One day when I was in elementary school I did the unthinkable and spilled my milk! I can remember crying and crying because I felt I had just done the worse thing *ever.* Poor baby. That kind of thinking followed me right into my adulthood. I would not get set free from that kind of emotional bondage until I reverted to a lesson I learned while at work. As a working Psychology Nurse, I had to one day teach a class about emotions. Let me tell you, if you ever want to really learn a lesson just teach a lesson.

Have you ever met a person who seemed to have no emotions? If their feelings and emotions were hooked up to an EKG machine the image would be a flat line. On the other hand, have you met the person who was ridiculously over emotional about everything? Their EKG image would probably look like a picture of the Smokey Mountains filled with peaks and valleys. A medically trained professional in the Psychology field would read these EKGs and give people potential medical diagnosis. The A-personal subject might be diagnosed with major depression. The other personality might be diagnosed as manic depressive.

Nevertheless, there is a happy medium for all emotions. Understanding how to express your emotions is a must. Here are a few communication principles. There are four basic communication methods. They are Assertive, Aggressive, Passive, and Passive Aggressive.

1. **Passive:** According to the dictionary passive is defined as accepting or allowing what happens or what others do without active response or resistance. This is certainly the place where I started and the place I could very easily go back to. Thank God that even if I feel myself

sliding then my understandings of the

other principles kick in.

2. **Aggressive:** Ready or likely to attack or

confront. You've all met that person.

They are extremely difficult to get along

with and seem to be always angry about

something. Any little thing sets them off

and triggers their aggression. I have a

friend who has been like that for years.

Years ago, I remember saying too her if

what people do make you angry then

where is it in you that they keep finding

a place to hang their triggers. The

aggressive person must do some serious

soul searching. The aggressive person

and the Passive person are not too far

apart. Both of their personalities can very easily be being driven by inner pain.

3. **Passive Aggressive:** To a person who is exhibiting passive aggressive behaviors, the behaviors are so subtle that the person doing it may not even recognize it. It's kind of like the letter "B" in the word subtle. You never hear it in the pronunciation, but you can't spell it without using the letter "B". Although it's silent it still makes an impact. I want to bring clarity to this behavior to help make us aware of what it might look like. According to Wikipedia you may exhibit indirect expressions of hostility,

such as through procrastination, stubbornness, sullen behavior, or deliberate or repeated failure to accomplish task for which one is responsible.

4. **Assertive:** Wikipedia defines assertiveness as confidently self -assured and positive. This is the place where I learned to protect my feelings and emotions and to not feel quite so vulnerable to the world. Whenever we talk about getting one's feelings hurt you already know I'm the queen of that. Wait a moment thou! Before I start feeling bad about feeling bad I just heard God bring his word to my rescue once

again. I was wondering in my spirit if Jesus ever got his feelings hurt and the answer is a resounding YES! In fact, I can site two examples in the scripture. The first is recorded by the Prophet Isaiah when he said, "He is despised and rejected of men, a man of sorrows, and acquainted with grief (Isaiah 53:3)." So, does he understand us when our feelings are hurt? Yes, on every level. Not only does he know what it feels like to be hurt himself he is even sensitive to our hurts. Isaiah 53:4 says, "Surely he has borne our griefs and carried our sorrows." I can even look at an intricate detail in the scripture. I noticed the first scripture did not say he *was* despised, but it says he *is* despised. That would mean people are still giving him grief so we are serving a God who never forgets what it's like to be rejected. I want to bring one more scripture to mind that demonstrates just how much God understands our feelings. For those of us who have children, we know the great pain one would feel if you ever saw someone cause your child pain. Well our heavenly father is no different. When his son Jesus was crucified on that cross the bible says the veil of the temple was rent from Top to Bottom. Every time I read that scripture I imagine God wearing the veil as his

garment and him ripping it like the Hulk
rips his shirt each time he got extremely
angry. It would have been an act of pain
and grief. What would you have ripped
up if you witnessed someone causing
this level of pain to your child?

There was one other time in my life that I
can recall feeling tremendously hurt. I was in
the beginning stages of rehearsing for a major
stage play that I had written. The play was
called *Butterfly.* Just two or three weeks into
the rehearsal I was told that I had to stop the
show. *OH, THE PAIN!* It felt like someone had
just ripped my heart right out of my chest with
no anesthesia. For those of you who are very

creative people you understand what a spiritual experience it is to create anything. When you have laid on your face and asked God to give you creative and witty ideas you pay a dear price for that. And then to have someone just destroy that which you have sought God for?! And so, it was. It would not be for yet another whole year before the time would come around again to do my play. But this time something was different. Let me show you how God can use your pain. The play called *Butterfly* is the story of a butterfly who got her wings broken by a character called Mean Old Mean Old Mr. Green. Although this was a children's story, the moral of the story was to teach kids that you cannot fly until you learn to forgive the person that broke your wings. I believe that in real life I was the butterfly. Did you ever know that a butterfly cannot make any sound? It's an animal that does not speak. How ironically consistent this is with my own personality. I was a beautiful animal who could not even speak for herself. What happened however is the pain of that experience got translated into the characters of the play. That same Play eventually became my very first published Children's book and later was seen on stage in New York City's Off Broadway.

Words are so powerful. By now you have probably heard the false statement that sticks and stones may break your bones but words can never harm you. Nothing could be farther from the truth. Words are such a powerful entity. Look at what God says about the tongue. "Life and death is in the power of the tongue. The Word of God is quick and powerful and sharper than any two-edged toward, piercing even to the dividing asunder of soul and spirit, and of the joints and marrow and is a discerner of the thoughts and intents of the heart (Hebrews 4:12)."

A sharp tongue can destroy a person's very soul. Many people who have the gift of speaking boldly must constantly make sure they don't allow that gift to turn into a weapon. You've been given the gift for a purpose. How many times has someone's words pierced your very soul? The emotional scars that words can cause can never be healed with just a band aid like a physical wound. If time heals all wounds then surely this must apply to our emotional wounds.

Here is a little help for those who have a sharp tongue. It is imperative that you stop and think about the repercussions of the words you are about to say. Most of the time when we say something that is intentionally meant to hurt we really don't care about the result because the intent is to hurt. But the thing I want you to consider is that words can never be removed from the atmosphere once they are spoken.

There was a demonstration done to show the physical results of this. A boy was asked to put nails in a fence each time he got angry, and then later remove the nails when he felt better. When he looked back at the fence now the nails were all gone but the open wounds caused by the nails would be there indefinitely. Can you now see how your words can impact a person?

Now, for those who feel they have been wounded by the words of others let's take this into consideration. A prayer called the Serenity Prayer was taught to me years ago. One of the most powerful lines in that prayer relates to being at peace with the things you cannot change. One of the many things we cannot

change in life is the words that other people
speak. Although we can't change their words
we can change our response to the words. No
warrior would ever go into a battle without their
shield. He knows that the purpose of his shield
is to deflect any arrows aimed at him. So, it is
in life. We must always be prepared to hold up
our shield. So, what are our shields? One is the
breast plate of righteousness. This shield--when
worn correctly—will guard you against the
brunt of the impact of negative words and
prevent you from retaliating.

It would behoove us to put on the whole
Armor of God, especially when dealing with
others. Gird your loins with the truth so

regardless of what is spoken you know the truth in your heart. Your feet should be shod with the gospel of peace just so you can still be at peace when hurtful words are spoken. Keep your shield of faith up to quench the fiery darts of negative words. The helmet of salvation will protect your mind, and your weapon for this battle will be the Sword which is the word of God.

Stuck in One Place in the Maze

All over the world there are people who may feel they are stuck in one place in the maze. Some may have been stuck just for weeks, some for months and some even for years. Being stuck in one place in the maze of Life can certainly stir up a multiplicity of emotions. Perhaps you feel sad, depressed, frustrated, in despair and even rejected by God. Watching others move along the maze who are taking the same route as you and surpassing you is certainly a double-edged sword. It has the potential to either inspire you to move on or send you spiraling into an abyss of what ifs. What if I started earlier? What if I had majored in something different in college? What if I had more money? What if I knew more people? What if I could just start all over again? It's bad enough to know that there are walls in the maze that often hinder or simply delay your progress. But then every-now-and-then you see yourself move up. The frustration in this movement comes when you realize you are moving up, but there seems to be a glass ceiling. *Ugggh!* Who knew the maze of Life had a ceiling as well? So, there you stand again *stuck.*

I confess. I was once the one who was stuck. With a tremendous love for working with children I had this desire to open a daycare center for years. I relentlessly researched the subject on how to open a center. I became that person who had all the knowledge, but nothing tangible to show for it. Perhaps one of the most disheartening things about it was to find a good location for a center and then watch someone else start the same business in the place you dreamed about. An even more disheartening thing was to watch that happen *over and over and repeatedly*. You never get immune to it. If you live with that desire for a dream you always feel the emotions attached to the joys and or pains of it. Once again, a day would come that I would cross paths with a woman who seemed to be living my dream. My own dreams grew from wanting to open just a regular daycare center to wanting to open the *KIDDS Center for Youth Development and Performing Arts*. In my vision, I saw a building with a dance studio, game room, indoor and outdoor basketball, piano room, art room, voice room, and a computer room with video games just for starters.

You Can Get There from Here | Pat Martin

I can still remember the night came when my daughter asked me to accompany her to a place where she would teach a private dance lesson to a student. I'm not sure why she insisted that I go with her, but I did. As I walked through the facility I was thinking, "What a nice place!" I stayed a little longer and propped up near the door in the private class room. And my daughter over heard me speaking out loud. When she asked what I was saying, I wasn't talking to her. Would you believe that I was just dreaming out loud? I pretended for a moment that this facility was my dream place and I spoke to the imaginary parent at the door and told her that the singing class was next door. I wasn't losing my mind. I was just day dreaming. Then the thing that took me back to that uncomfortable emotional place happened. I was introduced to the owner. She was everything wonderful you could imagine. She began to share her story with me. She too was a nurse who had a vision. She started right where she was at work and in just nine months could leave her job. Now just nine years later she stood in the very midst of her very vibrant and very much alive dream.

On our way, home my daughter said to me, "Don't be down mom," but I wasn't just down. I was more on an emotional roller coaster. On the low end of discouragement, I thought about what she had accomplished in just nine years and I was now on my thirtieth year of just dreaming. On the high, it was the most inspiring thing I could have ever encountered.

I ultimately left there thinking, "If God could do it for her he could surely do it for me." When I was a little girl we used to play a silly game with the water hose. We would take the hose and let the force of the water create a hole pulling the hose deeper and deeper into the ground. After a while the hose would be so deep that it would become stuck and no one could pull it out. The only way to get the hose unstuck was with a shovel. This compares to a great life lesson. Feelings of sadness and despair can flow for so long that they take us deeper and deeper into a place we can get stuck in. It is in this case that we must create a greater emotional shovel to dig us out. Hope, joy, and inspiration are a few of those tools that can dig us out of those places. I thank God for that encounter because it showed me two things. It showed me the magnitude of what God can do in a little bit of time. On the other hand, I saw myself being used by God once again. As the lady represented what can happen when God does a quick work. My life would now be a strength and encouragement for the people who are still waiting on God to move.

I encourage you to keep holding on. "God is not a man that He should lie (Numbers

23:19)." He has promised us that, "If we delight ourselves in him He would give us the desires of our hearts (Psalm 37:4)." Tell yourself, "It's Coming!" Now get back on your grind and keep pushing beyond your feelings. Don't be like the man digging the tunnel that got frustrated and gave up not knowing just one more dig and he would have gotten his breakthrough. *YOUR BREAKTHROUGH IS JUST AROUND THE BEND. KEEP PRESSING!*

6

The Journey

Life is a journey filled with hills and valleys, twists and turns. The hills and valleys somehow don't feel as challenging as the twist and turns because it's far more difficult to see what's around a corner than it is to look up or down to anticipate what's ahead. Just imagine a day on your journey as you move along. You hit a curve going one hundred miles an hour and someone takes the steering wheel away from you. That describes a moment I recently experienced in life.

July 29th at 11:00 AM a man steps into a waiting room and I hear my name called, "Mrs. Martin." If I never rejoiced over the calling of my name before I surely rejoiced then. I was about to go in to be prepped for a long awaited surgical procedure. My family was there to support me. We were all excited because we knew how this procedure would change my life for the rest of my life. For thirty years prior to this day I had been suffering from Achalasia. That rare condition I spoke of previously that would not allow me to swallow food, less enjoy life at a bare minimum at all. Now you don't have to have any medical training to understand the magnitude of the impact of not being able to eat. Surely for me this is a day to rejoice!

I got on that surgical table. A facemask was placed over my face for the anesthesia that would put me in another world. Only a few moments seemed to transpire and I felt myself being wheeled to recovery. Something's not right. I overheard a nurse saying, "Is this the lady who was supposed to have the surgery?" Oh Lord, what went wrong? I was still a little in the twilight zone so I couldn't comprehend anything anyone was saying. At that same moment, the doctor had gone into the waiting room to speak to my family and he said these *life changing* words, "I'm sorry, but when we got in she started to bleed and we feel we found a Malignant Cancerous Lesion."

PUMP THE BREAKS!!! Stop the car! Pull over! This was not on my life's journey plan. The doctor had just taken away my steering wheel and I was feeling that out of control feeling as if having lost control of a moving vehicle. Suddenly, my husband had the task of giving me the news. As he repeated the words from the doctor to me, my spirit pulled over to a rest stop. In a matter of fact state, I took in the information. I looked up at the faces of my daughters and saw their eyes filled with tears. Little did I know at that moment that their tears would become the fuel to jet me beyond this moment.

The doctors sent me home with the statement that they would not get the results of the biopsy back until the following Tuesday. This was *four days* away. My life's vehicle was now *stuck.* I was stuck in the maze of Life with no direction. *FOUR DAYS* of not knowing for sure! *Four days* came and went, but still no answer. Four days turned into six days. It's sheer torcher not knowing for days if you will live or die.

"YOU ARE HERE"

At this point it felt like I was in the very center of my maze holding a sign that said, "You are here." I was in the very depths of the core of my maze. So, deep in fact, that I could not see any way out. I had no idea where the exit was. So deep I could not see the entrance nor could I remember how I even got to this place. It was within those six days—right at this place—that my life took on a metamorphosis. I can remember it was on that Wednesday while I was listening to a song called, *He's Able*. I was suddenly overwhelmed with the image of my children in tears. I fell on my face and cried out to God like never before. I remembered the scripture from Romans 5:5 which says, "My hope would not be put to shame." Then I remembered Isaiah 55:11 where God said, "My word will not return void." Ultimately, I remembered that years ago He promised me that this sickness would not be unto death. I walked around the house singing, "My hope is built on nothing less than Jesus' blood and righteousness." With every passing moment, I began to renew my strength and with the vision of my two daughters' tears I refueled myself to now stop planning to die, but to live.

I even decided to use the title *Romans 5:5* to label the hospital call on my caller ID. I figured that whatever they said when they did call would have to come through the word of God. My vehicle for life was totally overhauled and ready to get back on the road. Thursday at 9:16 AM the call came. The voice of the nurse said, "Mrs. Martin, we got your pathology report back and the result is *NO Cancer.*"

I pray that my story empowers someone else to pullover, rejuvenate your spirit, take back your steering wheel and get back on your life's journey. *It ain't over til God says it's over.* In the meantime, you keep pressing forward on your journey even if you must do it unsure. Do it with uncertainties. Do it with handicaps. Move forward with whatever resources you have. Do it when you feel great,

and move on when you feel sick as a dog.
Don't let what appears as inadequacies impede
your progress in this maze called Life.

I was inspired recently when I read a
portion of the life story of Mozart. Mozart
heard music with a deformed ear and played
music with deformed fingers. By the age of 17
he had written 26 symphonies. Don't let what
seems like your imperfection or deformity stop
you from doing what you know God has called
you to do. God will perfect your imperfections
for his purpose.

The Bible tells the story of a man named
Mephibosheth. He was the son of Jonathan,
King David's friend. Mephibosheth was

dropped by his nurse as a child and the fall resulted in both of his feet being deformed. Even though he was deformed Mephibosheth received great favor from the King and ate at the Kings table. From this story, you can know in your heart that despite your shortcomings you have received tremendous favor from God. Many people have slowed down their route and become sidetracked on their Journey just because they did not feel like they had everything they needed to make the trip. I have often said all you have is all you'll ever need. Somehow God has a way of adding to what we have to make what we have sufficient.

Any man going on a journey understands there must be some type of preparation before the journey takes place. That's common sense. One item of preparation needed for the journey is fuel and that fuel may come in the form of rest and good nutrition. Nobody wants to set off for a journey in a broken-down vehicle. Continuously refuel and prepare yourself for the Journey every step of the way.

Now I'm about to stand on my healthcare soapbox for just a moment. With so very many health issues in the area of digestive dysfunctions it of course impacted my nutritional status. Anything that impacts the quality of your nutrition will certainly have a domino effect. Good nutrition is the foundation for fueling your physical body to make the Journey for Life.

Going Nuts

So, during my journey I'm not even certain what made me want to check, but I was led to check my blood pressure. You already know it's been called the silent killer, but I must have heard something because I moved on my unction to check my pressure. In doing so I found it to be slightly elevated. I have never had any problems with high blood pressure in the past and to the contrary it had always been on the little bit lower than normal side. So, on the day I found my pressure to be 150/100 I was shocked. Believe the literature that tells you there are no symptoms because I felt none. I admit that it did scare me a little to see my pressure like that. I am a nurse so I already know the impact high blood pressure can have on one's physical body. After monitoring my pressure for several days, I knew it was time to check in with my doctor once again.

On the day that I went to see my doctor she was away on vacation. How dare she take a vacation knowing that I needed her? Right? I guess this is proving my point that everyone needs rest on their Journey. So, since she was away a different doctor saw me on that day.

The new doctor did what your average doctor would do and immediately ordered yet another medication for me. Now my children know that even though Mommy is a nurse Mommy hates taking medicine. I mean I don't even take an aspirin for a headache. I just ride it out. Feeling a bit frustrated with the new doctor's bedside manner, I sat in the parking lot for a while before I came to a conclusion. I went back in and cancelled my follow up appointment with her and then went home with a new decision in my head and in my heart. My new decision was *I'M GOING NUTS!* Wait a minute. Before you call the authorities, let me explain. I remembered that this was *MY* Journey and I decided to take control since I had the following information.

I know. I know. It appears that I'm actually going nuts! I went into the Doctor's to check one thing, but ended up listening to a conglomeration of things. Then I went home and started to really re-think the Doctor's conversation with me. DISCLAIMER: I AM NOT A DOCTOR, but I am a Nurse just taking care of my own body so the things I'm about to say are not to be used as health advice for you. Remember, this is just *MY* Journey.

I left my western doctor thinking about eastern medicine and its alternatives. I didn't want to add another pill to my life. I began thinking about the fact that I never crossed paths with an obese Asian doctor giving me health advice, but it happens in America too frequently. Then when I got home I was reading that a folic acid deficiency can cause low hemoglobin. So, foods like green leafy veggies and liver or broccoli can increase your red blood cells. *WHY WOULDN'T THAT DOCTOR SAY THAT?* If you know a patient has had a long history of digestive problems perhaps the issue is more related to nutrition.

Western medicine is so disconnected. Everybody is treating a different part of the body, but nobody is talking together about how one thing affects another thing all in the *SAME*

BODY! We must stop just allowing our doctors to add more medicines without first considering what another doctor already has you on. As a Nurse, I have witnessed this too many times. So, I started to get my healthy eating on and found that nuts were good for a host of nutritionally healthy benefits. That's why I started going *nuts* and I'm a little *fruity* too. Ok. Ok. I know, but "Laughter is good like a medicine."

Now that you allowed me to take that turn in the maze I want to put us back on course by saying this. Occasionally something that seems to take you off course on your journey may be the very thing that gets you back on track. Do remember my point at this juncture is to reiterate the importance of rest and good nutrition for your journey.

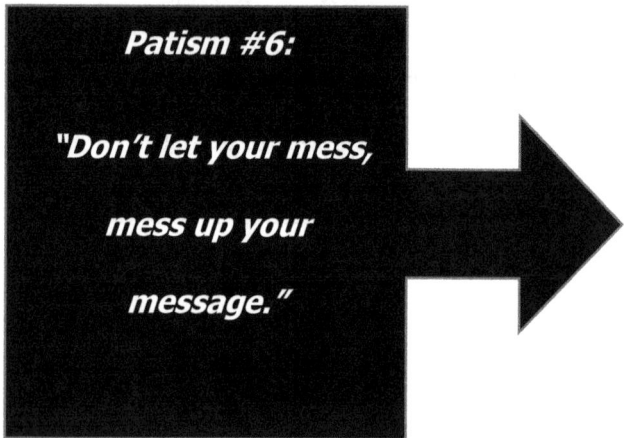

> **Patism #6:**
>
> **"Don't let your mess, mess up your message."**

One thing to keep in mind as you take your journey is that others are always watching you. They watch particularly closer each time you come up against a wall in your maze. Onlookers want to know how you handle the obstacles. There may have been a time when you have advised and encouraged others how to handle those same walls of despair or discouragement. *Don't let your mess, mess up your message.* Be careful not to let your actions and behaviors during your smooth times bring a negative reproach against the messages you have been sending to others.

In this new era of social media, we tend to take everyone along with us through our mazes. Bystanders tend to take a digital seat watching every little move that we make scrutinizing any inconsistencies between what we say and what we do. A picture still paints a thousand words. Unfortunately, we can't control whose words get set as the closed caption for our photos. Assumption is a dangerous treacherous weapon. It's therefore best that we not open that door as we travel this journey.

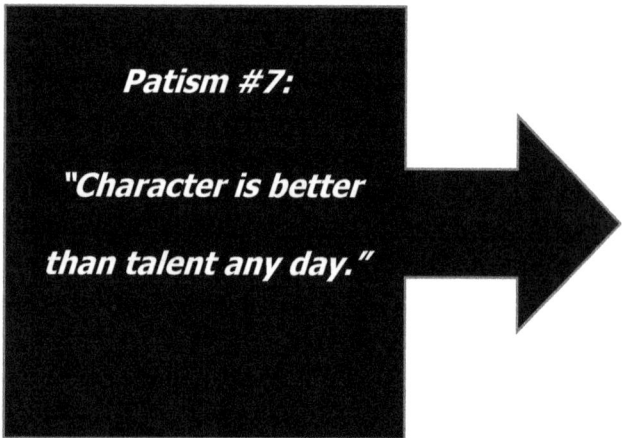

Patism #7:

"Character is better than talent any day."

That door can remain shut by the simple act of consistency in character. My perpetual motto for life is that, "Character is better than talent any day." When your character is

consistent then people are more likely to give

you the benefit of the doubt even if they observe

you doing or saying something out of character

for you. For those who feel that it's nobody's

business what you do on your social media

platforms you may want to consider this. Favor

with God, favor with man. Not only is it *good*

to have favor with both, but that favor can very

well make a difference in you progressing

through your Life's various level of mazes. The

distance between you and your success is Favor.

Patism #8:

"The distance between you and your success is Favor."

The up side of social media is that it does allow us to share our journeys with the world. The down side is that what we do share is sometimes one dimensional and not really the truth about our journeys. You know what's an interesting phenomenon I have noticed during my course as a Nurse? I've noticed that a patient who has a deadly disease will go on with their lives and function just fine before they find out their diagnosis. Then the moment the doctor goes in with the bad news, that's the moment the patient usually takes a turn for the worse.

One thing for sure, a maze is filled with choices and it's always up to the person in the maze which turn they will take. Now just like I've seen people take that left turn and spiral on a downhill slope I've also seen the opposite. Choices.

I recently saw a major television personality speaking and sharing how she had both liver and breast cancer, but overcame. We all saw a former American president fight a battle with brain cancer and come out victorious. Then just today I saw a woman just receive the news of having three tumors in her breast. She received the news by cutting her own hair and planning a party for herself.

At some point, you have to ask yourself the question, "What made the difference for these people?" Does cancer or any other disease have an aversion to a positive attitude? Can somebody with a winning spirit win? The mind is a powerful thing and I believe that God has given us the power to take control of our journeys with our minds. With God in our lives He gives us the direction, He orders our steps, and decides the final destination. It's a comforting thought to know that we are not alone on this journey.

"For as he thinketh in his heart so is he (Proverbs 23:7)." So, what kind of thoughts are you thinking? While on this journey make every effort to keep your thoughts positive and clear. Even when the road looks dark and you can't see your way. Just know that God is with you. Avoid negative thoughts and negative people at all cost. You know who the negative people are. They find fault in everything and everyone. They never have anything good to say. Their negativity comes from deep within and could be a byproduct of deep seated feelings or childhood traumas. Whatever the reason is, don't get caught up in their web. Choose your friends carefully. Connect with people who are going places. Their momentum will impact you in a positive way. It's hard to just be stagnant and stand still when others around you are being progressive. Connect with people who believe in your dreams and are willing to support your vision along the way.

Now that you have your fuel, a vehicle, and company for the journey there's one more thing you need. No one wants to go on a journey without having a destination. For your journey, today the word destination can be translated to the word *purpose*. You've heard this word many times before. Often people spend an entire life time looking for it. Sometimes we even become like little children who cry from the back seat, "Are we there yet?"

This book is certainly a demonstration of the twist and turns one can possibly take on the journey to purpose.

Everybody has a story to tell. We clearly understand all the obstacles that have or can occur on the way, but we all want God to make our purpose just as clear. If we can think about the possible things that could go wrong then surely, we can begin to think of the things that could go right. The good news is that there are no limitations to our dreams. We really can do or become whatever we desire.

Steps to Finding Your Purpose:

➢ Take out a paper and pen and make a list of everything you are good at doing.

(Remember that just because we are good at a thing does not mean you want to make a career out of it.)

> Narrow your original list down to the things you really enjoy doing.

> Now narrow the list again to the things you would do without pay.

> Connect with someone who is doing the thing you want to do.

> Invest in yourself. You've had a dream for years, stop talking about it and do it.

> Don't quit your day job until you have a comparable income from your dream.

There is a Purpose in Everything

I don't believe for one moment that anything on this earth just happens. I believe that God has systematically orchestrated every moment and every second of time. Nothing happens without His omniscience. His omnipresence allows Him to be there when it happens and His omnipotence causes whatever happens to work for good. "To everything there is a season and a time to every purpose under the heaven (Ecclesiastes 3:1)."

Today I know that the pain I endured during those six days of wondering if I would live or die were a part of God's master plan for me. When I came out on the other side I began to feel what God's purpose was for me. God had already confirmed me as a speaker of his word, but now He had given me a new message. He had just given me a life situation that would demonstrate His word in a manner that many others would be able to relate to. Let me revert to the moment during those days that God brought the two scriptures to me. The Lord saw me holding on to my hope for dear life. I was hoping and praying every moment that God would turn this thing around. I know God heard my prayers because He sent me to Romans 5:5. The words of the scripture would read, "And hope does not put us to shame because God's love has been poured out into our hearts through the Holy Spirit, who has been given to us." The day I got this word from God I was giving it my all to try to keep my countenance up in the presence of my family and friends. I didn't want to just sit home sulking every day, so one day I agreed to ride with my daughter to her rehearsal. She was just about done with her rehearsal so I sat in the car alone waiting. During that wait God and I had a conversation about hope. When He spoke Romans 5:5 to me He made it clear that if I would hold on to the hope that everything would be alright then it would. He knew He had to make it so because He was not going to allow me to be shamed by having hope in his word. And on the sixth day I spent that morning in the epitome of emotional distress. I was a basket case. I cried until there were no more tears. I laid out with my face in the carpet crying out to God. And every time I saw that image again of the face of my children in tears it sent me deeper into despair. Just the thought of them having to go through losing their mother was unbearable. *WHY GOD WHY!*

At my breaking point God comforted me with His words from Isaiah 55:11, "So shall my word be that goeth forth out of my mouth. It shall not return unto me void but it shall accomplish that which I please and it shall prosper in the *thing* whereto I sent it."

If you will note in this scripture in the King James Version the word *THING* is written in italics. The significance of that is to bring our attention to that word. Any time a word is written in italics in the scriptures means that the

italicized word was not the original word

written in the Bible's original translation. Now

I don't know what the original word for *THING*

was, but what I do know is this. One day I had

a *THING*, but God had a word for my *THING*.

It was clear now what God wanted me to do.

How could I be so selfish to think this was all

just about me and my victory?

There are many others today with a

THING. Somebody reading this book right now

is right in the midst of a *THING* with little hope.

But God would have me to tell you today that

THERE IS HOPE FOR YOUR THING. There is

NO- thing that the enemy can create that God

doesn't have a word for. Hold on to God's word. Hold on to your hope. Remember He said, "His word would *prosper in the thing.*" Which do you think has more power God's word or the *thing*? Right! God's power!

God wanted me to tell the world that He has a word for whatever the *thing* is. It is through all my Life's twists and turns in the maze of Life that God used this to birth the Hope & Truth Women's Conference and this book. There was purpose after all. And there is purpose after all you're going through right now.

7

The Way Out

There is Hope for your situation as well as a way out of your Maze. These principles are proven to be effective for the directions to the exit of any maze.

1. ***Allow yourself to be guided:***

   Good Godly advice can be obtained when you connect yourself with good Godly people. It is so true that like poles attract, often when we find ourselves traveling the mazes with others who have not made that spiritual commitment, we sometimes take on their behaviors. It is often a situation where the blind is leading the blind. You will never get out of the maze of life staying connected to the spiritually blind. Pray that God will give you insight. Insight is far better than your eyesight because your natural eyes will often deceive you. Everything that glitters is not gold. Those are not my words; however, the deception of the enemy would have us to believe that. Know that the grace of God can surely lead us and guide our paths. "The steps of a good man are ordered by the Lord (Psalm 37:23)."

2. ***Be open to constructive criticism***:

The Spirit of God will reveal to your spirit
which criticism spoken are constructive.
"Beloved believe not every spirit, but try the
spirits whether they are of God (1 John
4:1)." A true man or woman of God will
have the integrity to know what to say to us,
how to say it and when to say it. Timing is
everything. God knows when we are ready
to receive that which we may otherwise
reject. Many others may have already
traveled the pathways we choose. Wisdom
is a precious gift and the wisdom that comes
to prevent our falls is priceless. There is
nothing more valuable than being able to
glean from someone who has already been

through that level or type of maze and already knows the way out.

3. ***Be Grateful:*** To get out of the wandering maze you will need tools. Gratitude can be one of the most powerful tools you can have while in the maze. This tool is most effective when used right in the very place where you are. To the working world I say, that job you're complaining about is the same job somebody else is praying for. To the married I say again, that spouse that you are finding intolerable right now could be the gem of a life time for someone else. We must find a way to activate our tool of

gratitude. It has been proven time and time again that our attitude is the key to engaging our gratitude. Here are some instructions; take your attitudes about life and stack them one on top of the other. Once they are all stacked high then place your gratitude on top of them. Now you must climb to the top of that stack. At this point, standing on your gratitude will now give you a different vantage point by which to look at everything around you. Now you can see things from a whole different perspective. Can you imagine being able to see over the top of the walls of the Maze. What an advantage this now gives you. You may still not be able to see all the way through but you will certainly gain a little better clarity and understanding about where you are. This will help give you direction and show you how and where to make your next step.

4. *Do it Now:*

A real determined persons clock does not have numbers, just the word *NOW* because there's no time greater than the present. Procrastination is the enemy of the people and there are several ways to thwart its evil presence. Good time management is the kryptonite of Procrastination. My personal philosophy is that you may get your money back but you can never get your time back.

Patism #9:

"Your tomorrow is today!"

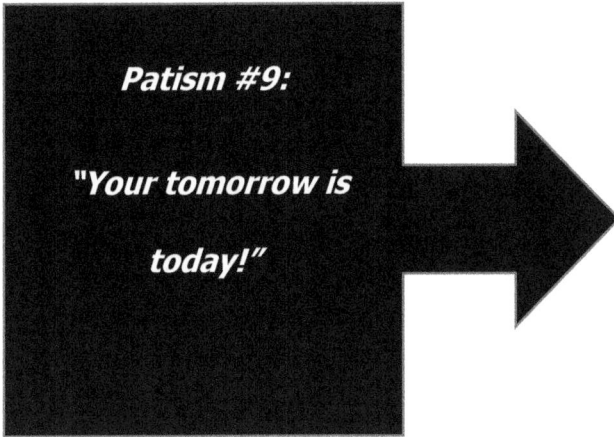

On the day that you decide to move forward and progress from where you are in the maze you must actually move. A second kryptonite to Procrastination is having an accountability partner. A great partner will not allow you to stand stagnate in the place where you are, knowing there is greater for you ahead. Do you recall the day you said, "I will do it tomorrow?" Well, your tomorrow is today. God himself works on a different timeline than

man. We work by time and God works by
timing.

Somebody's great grandmother said,
"Cleanliness is next to Godliness." When I
become a great grandmother, I'm going to
change that to, "Timeliness is next to
Godliness." Did you not ever hear that he is an
on-time God? As much as I love humor I don't
mean that in any humorous way. Punctuality is
not to be taken lightly. Chronic tardiness can be
interpreted as a latent form of narcissism. It is a
blatant disrespect for others who wait for you.
It may also simply be a form of denial. Perhaps
the chronically late never perceive the impact

that their tardiness has on them and those around them.

During the maze God can anticipate the occurrences that we cannot. His scriptures tell us that, "He will cause all things to work together for good." Only the God of time can strategize our lives so that the things coming around those corners inside those mazes hit us at a time when He has orchestrated it to.

Now that you understand the power of *NOW*, move forward! Write that book! Change your career and stop doing that thing that you dread every day. Go ahead, start that business! Make new empowering relationships! DO IT NOW! Even though you just got this new found burst of confidence and motivation you may still be asking yourself the question, "What next? What do I do from here?" A great analogy here might be seeing one who is in a dark room. You have everything it takes to get out except the direction and support. So now let's get those two things in motion. It's always easier to move about when there is light. If you attempt moving forward in the dark by just feeling your way around it could cause you to stumble. Save yourself the potential pain by allowing someone in to shed light on the subject. Find someone who is doing the thing that you want to do. Watch them. Learn from them. Learn from their mistakes and learn from their successes. Having an accountability partner is like being given the key to a door that has had you locked

in. I cannot begin to tell you how priceless that

is. Let me at least try to help you understand

how valuable that really is.

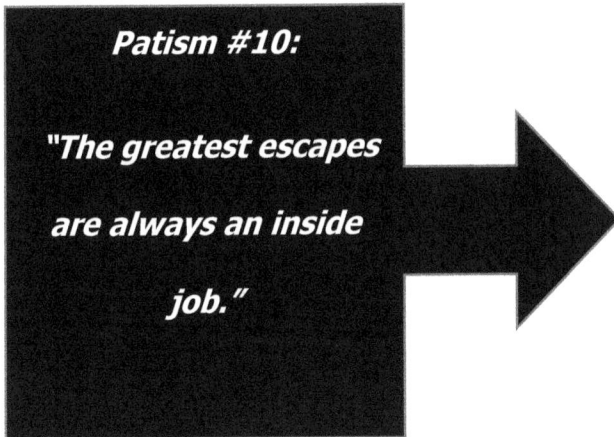

Patism #10:

"The greatest escapes
are always an inside
job."

One night while working a night shift on

my nursing job, I found myself staring at the

door to the room where I was doing private

duty. As I looked at that door I felt a sense of

imprisonment. Of course, I could have just walked right out, but not at a tremendous loss of income. Speaking of gratitude, I had expressed many times how grateful I was to have a job with minimal physical & mental labor for optimal pay. This was surely the job many people prayed for. But that night I realized that there was greater. There was something for me beyond that door. I continued to stalk that door thinking about its physical structure. It was only two inches thick. *TWO INCHES!* Was that all there was standing between me and my destiny? Were the walls of this portion of my maze just two inches thick? I actually took a picture of the door that night and I keep it on my phone as a reminder that there is not as much between me and my destiny as I sometimes imagine. Guess what? Every door you stand behind is only two inches as well. Don't let your hopes and dreams get stuck behind the doors.

God eventually sent me the keys in the form of an accountability partner. She would put words in my spirit that opened every potential hindrance to me moving to that next level. After just one conversation with her I garnered the strength and determination to do things I never thought I could do. My life was now on fast forward. When I saw myself excelling I admit I was surprised at myself. Moving forward had taken me to a place in the maze that I had never been. It allowed me to

see new things and new perspectives. I actually

started having a positive impact on others who

were near me and that was a good thing. It

appears that confidence and progress are

contagious.

Follow Your Instincts

There is an inner man within you that

will speak to you and give you directions along

the way. He or she will give you that *gut feeling*

that I spoke of before, and that feeling will turn

into a knowing. The more we listen to the

direction of the inner man the less we must seek

council from the outside. The relationship with

your inner man must be restored. We are often

lost in the maze of life simply because we've refused to give ear to that inner voice.

The inner voice is well versed in all the levels and dimensions of the maze. It has seen every entrance and exit. That means it can tell long before hand if you are about to even enter a certain part of the maze or not. The inner man knows what behaviors will lead us to paths of destruction and darkness. It knows every exit of every compartment of the maze. It has the far sight to see where every path will take us. It knows when the paths are the passages to destruction or to our destiny. Even if we choose the wrong direction the inner man can help get us back on track and back to the places where

God intended for us to go. The inner man has
an instinct like an animal that has lost its way
and traveled far off course, but somehow that
same animal can still find its way back home. It
may even take years but it can still happen.
That's the kind of spiritual sense of direction
God has given each of us.

     I know personally what it feels like to be
lost. Unfortunately, I have a very poor sense of
direction. I can recall a time that my daughter
took me on a trip with her. I felt honored
because she is a touring musician and invited
me to go along on one of her nearby trips.
While she was rehearsing I could go visit my
family in the same city. After my short visit, it

was time to go to the place where my daughter

was rehearsing. With an address and a GPS in

hand I began the drive back. As the voice on

the GPS began to say, "You have arrived at your

destination," I felt such pride and confidence

because I made it! Little did I know at that

point I was not anywhere near the place I was

supposed to be. I reached out to my daughter

and for the next solid hour I rode around and

around in circles. I even asked people for the

location and no one seemed to know what I was

even talking about. I was lost in a maze.

What an awful feeling knowing that you

have no idea where you are or how to proceed.

Not only was I now flustered to tears but my

daughter could no longer concentrate clearly on her music knowing her mother was lost in the city with no sense of direction. As bleak as the situation seemed, God had a plan. Eventually my daughter spoke some words to me that I can hear God speaking to many of you who are lost in the mazes of life right now. She eventually said to me, "*Just be still and I will come and get you.*" I can't begin to tell you what relief I felt having heard those words. No longer did I have to depend on my own intuition. I knew help was on the way! Hear me when I say that God has already told us to, "Be still and know that He is God." You can breathe a sigh of relief. I simply had to call upon my daughter and I got what I needed. Call upon the name of the Lord and He will surely hear you and answer. In fact, even as you read the words of this book and allow His word to enter your spirit He is already on His way. I hear God saying, "You're about to come out!"

Be Patient on The Journey

We have all heard the infamous question asked by most children on a journey, "Are we there yet?" There is nothing more frustrating for a child than to be on a journey and not know where they are going or if they have arrived. When I think about it, that question may be more annoying to the parent than it is for the child. That makes me wonder if God gets annoyed with us asking when we will arrive at our destination. Ha! His frustration may come in knowing like a parent that the journey itself is a process, but we'll get there eventually. We must all learn to be a little more patient with the process.

I suppose even Moses experienced this with the Children of Israel who grew weary of the journey taking so very long. There were times when the Israelites complained so much on the journey that Moses took their complaints to God. Even though God met many of their immediate requests, I don't believe it hurried the process much. We may get things to appease us for the interim, but those things can often put us in Gods permissive will verses His perfect will.

Don't let your impatience cause you to get short changed from the ultimate thing that God really desires for you. Remember sometimes the shortcut just may be the long way around.

Set a Goal

Long before you find yourself in a maze it's vitally important that you have a goal in mind. That way even if you get lost along the way you can at least remember where you were going in the first place. You will also be able to tell someone else what your goal is just in case you have to ask for directions along the way. Setting a feasible goal is good for the psyche. It is even better when you set short term goals along the way. Reaching short term goals helps to keep you encouraged toward your ultimate goals.

Imagine a traveler making the journey from Florida to California. Can you imagine how overwhelming and discouraging it would be to get just one sign for the whole journey that said California 3000 miles? Thank God for small signs along the way. These signs direct us as well as give us that psychological boost that we are almost there.

Now let me boost your faith just a little bit. This is particularly for those of you who have set goals that others around you don't feel are probable or even possible for you. I recently heard a report about the eleven college careers that frequently do not get jobs. Without even knowing the list, it's discouraging to think that a person who made the sacrifice for higher education would now become the sacrificial lamb. For every career on that list somebody defied the odds and became a success at the thing the statistics said would not work. A mindset of determination always has the power to override and supersede the odds. Reaching a difficult goal takes a dogmatic approach.

The best biblical demonstration of this I can think of is the one demonstrated by Queen Esther. I simply love her words, *"If I perish then let me perish."* This was one determined woman. You hear me? She had a goal in her head and it did not matter what anybody said or thought. She set a goal that she was determined to achieve and she did it.

I'm kind of feeling that spirit of Esther right about now. Best-selling Author was one of the careers on the "No Fly" list for me. Somebody maybe should have told J.K. Rowling that while she was on welfare writing her first Harry Potter book. They should have also told the bumblebee he was on the "No Fly" list as well. Instead, he keeps right on flying and high above every obstacle or hindrance that comes its way.

Make it Happen

I cannot begin to tell you the level of determination it takes to make things happen. One must be willing to make sacrifices. It can call for sacrificing sleep, meals, relationships and especially any doubts. Let me tell you where I got this step from or should I say who I got it from.

On yet another occasion I made a promise to the kids in my dance program that was far bigger than even I could imagine. How I come up with these hair brain ideas I can't tell you. You know! Ideas like we're all going to *NEW YORK CITY FOR FREE!!!* Ha! Believe it or not it happened! But maybe the fact that it happened was strengthened by another hair

brain idea I had. Prior to going off on a tour bus

to New York I had already prepared our faith

and our perspective by telling the kids one day,

"We're performing at The Atlanta Civic

Center." And we did! So, New York City

wasn't so far-fetched after all. But wait a

minute, where was that $10,000 going to come

from? I really am a far more stable person than

that and it's not like me to be irrational. I had

BIG dreams. Boy did I ever have big dreams.

If God will do exceedingly, abundantly above

what I could ever ask or think then I can't

imagine what plans God might have for us next.

Once I made this grand announcement it was now on me to bring it to pass. I have often said when it comes to making plans for the kids' shows and seeing how hard they work then *NO* is not an option. I remember lying across my bed late one night toiling over the thought of having to raise $10,000 in two weeks. Then the moment came when I rolled over to face the television and saw a man named Les Brown. Les Brown said some words that rang in my spirit, "MAKE IT HAPPEN." One day I'm going to meet Les Brown and tell him this story. After he said those words I went to bed. I later got up the next morning with a new-found confidence. I picked up the phone and began to call people who I knew had money and confidently said, "I need $2000 from you, and $2000 from you, and $2000 from you. I kept the requests going. Two weeks later I was in the office of the Civic Center with a check for $10,000.

To this day I still operate my life on the *MAKE IT HAPPEN* theory. I have said, "Nothing is impossible with God," so much that a parent had the scripture engraved on a plaque with my name on it. "For with God nothing shall be impossible (Luke 1:37)."

Getting Out

Getting out of the maze can be just as complex as being in the maze. Remember the children of Israel wandering through the wilderness. They thought being in the wilderness was bad enough until they made it through to the Promised Land then the wars really began.

Please don't let me discourage you by telling you that there will be more battles to fight and more challenges waiting for you after you get out of the maze. The good news is just as the Israelites had to fight many battles God had already arranged for them to win. So just know whatever happens you will win in the end because God is with you.

Despite the complexities of the maze please know that you will make it in, through, and out. Let me leave you with these words of encouragement today. Regardless of any of Life's mazes know this: if there's a way in, there's always a way out. Keep going.

About the Author

Pat Martin is an American Pastor, Motivational Speaker, Author and Playwright. As Pastor of The Purpose Church she is *"Empowering People for Life."* Having worked for over thirty (30) years as a Registered Nurse, she has a focus in Behavioral Health. She has appeared twice on the nationally known Trinity Broadcasting Network, and has multiple appearances on various local and national television networks featuring her work with children and youth in the Arts.

As the Founder and Executive Director of the non-profit organization *KIDDS Dance Project* her work has been featured on MTV, VH1, Comedy Central, CBS, NBC, Teen Nick and the CW Channels. Her philosophy for life is that *"character is better than talent any day."*

@PatMartin | www.patmartinspeaks.com | (404) 539-6922

Dudley Publishing House

www.dphouse.net

www.ingramcontent.com/pod-product-compliance
Lightning Source LLC
Chambersburg PA
CBHW051815090426
42736CB00011B/1485

YOU CAN GET THERE FROM HERE

"MAKING IT THROUGH THE MAZES OF LIFE"

WRITTEN BY:
PAT MARTIN

Scripture quotations are taken from the *Holy Bible*, New Living Translation,
copyright ©1996, 2004, 2007 by Tyndale House Foundation; the *Holy
Bible,* King James Version. New York: American Bible Society: 1999 Holy
Bible, King James Version, copyright © 1999 by New York: Bible Society; and
the *Holy Bible,* Amplified Version, *Copyright © 2015.*

Printed in the United States of America

THIS BOOK IS NOT INTENDED TO BE A HISTORY TEXT. While every
effort has been made to check the accuracy of dates, locations, and historical
information, no claims are made as to the accuracy of such information.

For book orders, author appearance inquires and interviews, contact author:

ISBN- 978-0-9988025-3-4
ISBN-10: 0998802530

Dudley Publishing House

www.dphouse.net